(continued from front flap)

Contents include: Introduction to Computer Data Processing □ Representation of Information □ Introduction to Programming □ Introduction to the RPG □ Printer Output Vertical Format □ Printer Output Horizontal Format □ Extension and Summarization □ Multiple Card Types □ Multiple Inputs □ Tables □ Random Access □ Levels of Control □ Updated Tables □ Calculations □ Miscellany □ Examples

COMPUTER DATA PROCESSING
AND PROGRAMMING

PRENTICE-HALL INTERNATIONAL, INC., *London*
PRENTICE-HALL OF AUSTRALIA, PTY. LTD., *Sydney*
PRENTICE-HALL OF CANADA, LTD., *Toronto*
PRENTICE-HALL OF INDIA PRIVATE LTD., *New Delhi*
PRENTICE-HALL OF JAPAN, INC., *Tokyo*

COMPUTER DATA PROCESSING

AND PROGRAMMING

THOMAS R. GILDERSLEEVE

Vice-President
NGP and Associates, Inc.
Rowayton, Connecticut

Prentice-Hall, Inc., Englewood Cliffs, N.J.

Current printing (last digit):

10 9 8 7 6 5 4 3 2 1

13-165928-6
Library of Congress Catalog Card Number: 76-99959
Printed in the United States of America

To my wife, Beverly

PREFACE

This book is an introduction to computer data processing. Crucial to an understanding of this subject is the concept of computer programming. Computer programs are written in one of two types of languages:

1. Computer-oriented languages
2. Problem-oriented languages

A computer-oriented language retains in it the characteristics of the computer for which it is designed. Thus, a program written in a language oriented to computer X runs on that computer and on no other computer.

Problem-oriented languages have a high degree of computer independence. No programming language is completely computer independent, and a program written in a problem-oriented language for one computer will not, without modification, run on another computer. However, the amount of modification required is minor.

This book describes computer programming in terms of a problem-oriented language. The one chosen is the International Business Machines (IBM) Report Program Generator language. With a minor amount of modification, a program written in IBM Report Program Generator (RPG) language can be run on other manufacturers' computers.

Other problem-oriented languages are FORTRAN, COBOL, and ALGOL. FORTRAN and ALGOL are scientifically oriented languages. RPG and COBOL are business-oriented languages. The input/output operations in COBOL are *procedural*. That is, they are part of the language, and consequently a man writing a program can describe how he wants his input/output operations to occur. Input/output operations in RPG are not procedural. They occur in a fixed way. While this decreases the flexibility of the RPG language, it also simplifies it. A person can be trained to program in RPG language more quickly than in COBOL and, once trained, can write programs about twice as fast as someone trained in COBOL can write programs in that language. Consequently, RPG has appeal when it is desired to do things quickly or easily and is more applicable to straightforward processing than to complicated work. As a result, programs to read data, perform summary calculations, and print reports are often written in RPG language, and it is typically the only programming language used at installations whose only data-processing experience prior to the installation of their computers was with unit record equipment.

To repeat, this book's purpose is to serve as an introduction to computer data processing. In satisfying this purpose it becomes necessary to orient the reader to some programming language. The one chosen is RPG. Thus, this book also serves as an introduction to RPG programming. An attempt is made to be as clear in performing this second function as we hope to be in introducing the subject of computer data processing. This function is one of orientation only. The RPG programs appearing in the text of this book are fragmentary. No part has been included that is not pertinent to the subject for which the program serves as an example.* If after

---

*An exception to this statement is the example given in Chapter 16. This program has been successfully compiled and tested.

reading this book the reader desires to go on and write an RPG program for a specific computer, it is suggested that he get, from the computer's manufacturer, the RPG reference manual that describes the way the particular manufacturer has implemented the RPG language. This book should provide an understanding of RPG language that makes such reference manuals easier to employ.

In preparing this book, reference was made to several prior publications, which are listed here for acknowledgement purposes:

IBM SYSTEM/360 Operating System Report Program Generator Language (IBM publication C24–3337)

UNIVAC III UTMOST General Reference Manual (UNIVAC publication UP–3853)

UNIVAC 9200/9300 Systems Card Report Program Generator Reference Manual (UNIVAC publication UP–4106)

The material in Chapter 1 finds its genesis in the UTMOST manual. The example used in Chapter 12 comes from the IBM RPG manual. Chapter 16 is taken from the UNIVAC RPG manual.

T. R. GILDERSLEEVE

CONTENTS

COMPUTER DATA PROCESSING
AND PROGRAMMING

1 INTRODUCTION TO COMPUTER DATA PROCESSING

In most data processing, there is a type of data, called *master data*, that is a combination of descriptive and cumulative items. Names, addresses, badge numbers, pay rates, year-to-date gross, year-to-date withholding tax, and quarter-to-date Social Security tax are examples of master data representing the payroll area; stock numbers, descriptions, on-hand amounts, and units of measure represent the inventory-control area.

There is another type of data fed into most data-processing systems; this information reflects activity the monitoring of which is the function of the data-processing system. This type is *transaction data*. Hours worked, quantities shipped, and amounts invoiced are examples from, respectively, the areas of payroll, accounts receivable, and accounts payable.

Processing consists basically of applying the items of transaction data, either singly as they come up or in cumulative batches, to update the master data.

On the other hand, processing may also consist of periodical production of information from the master data alone. An example in the accounts-receivable area is the production of a monthly statement.

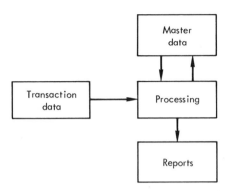

Figure 1-1   The general data-processing operation.

There is one other major item in the general data-processing operation—the report. In essence, the report is a by-product of the

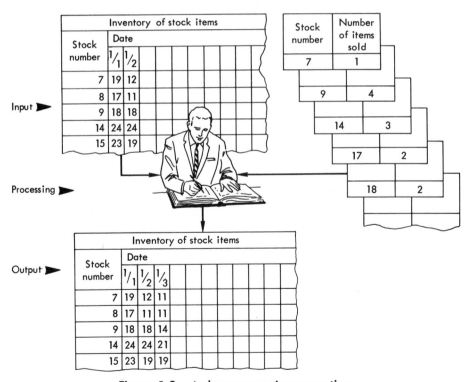

Figure 1-2   A data-processing operation.

processing operation in that it reflects, in summary or other form, the updating of the master data, which is the chief function of the data-processing system. However, for most purposes, the report can be considered the end product and therefore the most important of the four elements. It abstracts and highlights critical aspects of the business picture that judicious processing of transaction and master data uncovers, and it is looked to by management for necessary information for decisions in production, sales, purchasing, finance, and all other phases of business.

The schematic in Figure 1-1 relates the four basic elements in the general data-processing operation.

To further investigate the elements of a data-processing operation, examine the steps in the solution of a simplified processing application. Consider a company that keeps a record of its stock in a ledger. Each day a clerk is supplied with a pile of sales slips. On the basis of the slips, the clerk brings the inventory up-to-date by writing a new column in the ledger. A representation of this data-processing operation is shown in Figure 1-2.

As indicated in Figure 1-2, this data-processing operation breaks down into three parts.

1. Input: the information to be processed
2. Output: the information produced by the processing
3. Processing: the operations required to produce the output from the input

To do the processing represented in Figure 1-2, the clerk must go through a certain sequence of steps. One possible sequence is represented in Figure 1-3. To do the steps shown in this figure, the following is necessary.

1. The clerk must be able to do arithmetic (e.g., he must be able to subtract the sales quantity from the inventory quantity).
2. He must be able to make logical decisions (e.g., he must be able to determine whether or not there is a sales slip for a given product).
3. He must be able to remember information (e.g., after he subtracts the sales quantity from the inventory quantity he

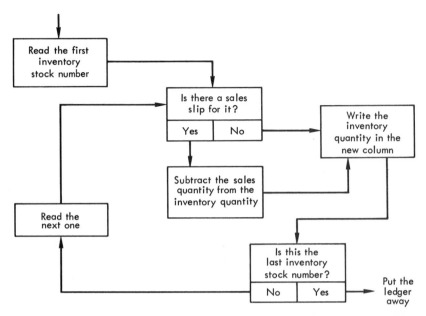

Figure 1-3   The sequence of steps in the data-processing operation.

must remember the difference until he writes it in the ledger).

4. He must do the steps in the sequence shown or do something logically equivalent to this sequence of steps.

These four elements of processing are referred to, respectively, as

1. Arithmetic
2. Logical decision
3. Memory
4. Control

Experience has determined that to do the general data-processing operation, input, arithmetic, logical decision, memory, control, and output are required. These six elements are shown in their logical relationship in Figure 1-4.

A data-processing system is a structure of people and equip-

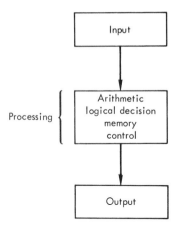

Figure 1-4   The elements of a data-processing operation.

ment whose purpose it is to perform the operations of input, arithmetic, logical decision, memory, control, and output in such a manner as to implement one or more data-processing applications of the organization to which the system belongs. In the material that follows, the nature of several different kinds of data-processing systems is investigated. The kinds of data-processing systems are

1. Manual
2. Manual with key-driven devices
3. Punched card
4. Computer

Also interwoven into the following material is a discussion of bulk data storage media other than punched cards—namely, paper and magnetic tape.

1-2
MANUAL DATA
PROCESSING

The above example is of a manual data-processing system. Typically, data is stored in such a system by being written on paper. Thus, the master data is written in the ledger and the transaction data on the sales slips. From time to time special reports may be generated on the basis of the information in the ledger—certainly reorders of stock would. However, since the ledger is already in a legible form, it also serves in many ways as a report in which the information is looked up directly. This is typical of the master data in a manual data-processing system.

With the advent of electronic data processing, it has become customary to describe data in terms of *files, records,* and *fields.* Although these terms are not typically used in manual data processing, the entities to which they refer are present in such systems. For example, in the simplified inventory described above, the ledger is the master file, and the pile of sales slips is the transaction file. A file is a set of related records. For example, each line in the ledger is a record for a particular stock commodity, and each sales slip in the pile is a record for a particular sale. A record is made up of a number of fields, all fields of a record containing related information. For example, each line in the ledger is made up of a stock number field and a series of stock-level-by-date fields. Each sales slip is made up of a stock number field and a number-sold field.

The illustration described above is also an example of *sequential data processing.* Sequential data processing generally requires some preparatory steps. For example, in the case of the above illustration, consider how the pile of sales slips is generated. During the day, each time a sale is made, a sales slip describing the commodity sold and the units of the commodity sold is prepared. At the end of the day, the clerk receives from the sales organization a bundle of sales slips, each representing a transaction. (For purposes of simplicity, assume that each transaction and consequently each sales slip involves only one commodity.) Before the clerk can run the slips against the ledger he must *sort* them, that is, put them into stock number order. Once he has put the slips into stock number order, he probably also finds it convenient to *summarize* the sales by commodity so that there is only one summary sales slip per stock number in the sales slip pile to be run against the ledger.

This sort of the transaction file before it is applied to the master file is typical of sequential data processing. The transaction file is sorted on the *key* of the transaction record. The key is a field or combination of fields in the transaction record. It is the key that is used to match up the transaction records with the master records to which they apply. For example, in the simplified inventory application, the stock number field is the key.

The clerk could have taken the bundle of sales slips as received from the sales organization and applied them to the ledger in the order in which they came up in the stack. Such an approach would require a logic different from the one shown in Figure 1-3 and would be an example of *random data processing*. The basic logic for a random updating of the ledger is shown in Figure 1-5.

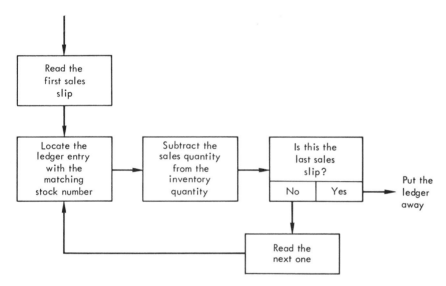

Figure 1-5   Random data processing logic.

To do random data processing, it must be possible to update a single master record without disturbing the other records in the master file. In terms of the manual inventory application, this means the ledger would have to be reorganized so that a single commodity line entry could be updated without the requirement to copy the inventory level amounts for all the other line entries.

In this example, the sales slips are collected during the day and then are applied in the resulting batch to the ledger at the end of the day. Consequently, this is an example of *batch data processing*. In a batch data-processing system, random data processing is hardly ever used. The reason for this is due to the fact that the search to locate the matching master record for each transaction record is generally more time consuming than to take the time to initially order the transactions by key and then apply the transactions to the master file. It is true that sequential data processing minimizes search time on the master file, as is shown schematically in Figure 1-6. As illustrated in this example, in sequential data

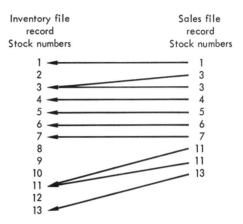

Figure 1-6   Minimizing search time by ordering files.

processing the records in the master file are accessed in sequence, and all transactions can be applied to the master records in just one pass over the master file.

The opposite of a batch data-processing system is a *realtime data-processing system*. If a realtime data-processing system were to be used for the simplified inventory application, each sales slip would be applied to the inventory ledger as soon as the sale it represents had been made. There are two requirements that must be met to institute a realtime data-processing system.

1. Since transactions can be expected to occur in random fashion with respect to key, it must be possible to do random data processing.
2. There must be a relatively rapid method of routing the transactions from their point of origin to the point at which the updating of the master file is to take place.

It is the magnitude of the logistics of trying to meet this second requirement that causes manual data-processing systems to typically be batch operations.

In doing the data-processing operation the clerk is following a procedure. In a well-run organization there is a procedure manual that describes the steps the clerk follows in updating the inventory. Then if the clerk is absent, another man can do the clerk's work by following the steps described in the procedure manual.

For an operation of low enough volume, the approach described above is adequate. It is possible for one clerk to keep the inventory records for the simplified inventory application up-to-date. However, as the volume of the company's operations increases, the burden of keeping the inventory records up-to-date will become too heavy for one clerk. It will be necessary to add other clerks to handle the increased work load. With the advent of a number of people to maintain the inventory records, management may adopt the procedure of breaking down the inventory maintenance into a number of steps and of assigning one person to each one of the steps. Thus, one clerk might *read* the sales slips, *sort* them into the same order in which the inventory commodities are listed in the inventory ledger, and *summarize* the sales slips by commodity. A second clerk might *subtract* the entries on the sales slips from the balances on hand and *record* the differences in the ledger.

This approach consists of breaking down the job into a number of tasks. These tasks fall into categories that constitute the functions of data processing.

1. Reading
2. Sorting
3. Calculating
4. Recording

When a job is simplified by breaking it down into a series of tasks, the data to be processed is circulated through this series. Each task is the responsibility of a single person who performs the task repeatedly on the continuing flow of data.

The approach just described is characteristic of manual data-processing systems. Analyzing a job and dividing it into a series of tasks is the first step in the evolution of data-processing systems. There is still a procedure to be followed in performing each task and in moving the data between tasks, and this procedure should be documented in a procedure manual.

1-3
KEY-DRIVEN
DEVICES

Some of the functions of data processing are mechanized in the typewriter and the adding machine. Each of these office machines performs one of the basic functions. Thus, the typewriter records, and the adding machine calculates.

Since the machines perform only one data-processing function, they are "building block" machines. They can fit into the pattern of analyzing a job into a series of tasks with no loss of flexibility. Their advantage lies in the fact that they increase both the speed and the accuracy of their operators.

The mechanization of data-processing functions is the second step in the evolution of processing systems. The procedure and the procedure manual remain.

1-4
PUNCHED-CARD
MACHINES

With the keyboard-operated typewriter or adding machine, the operator must act as an interpreter, taking the results produced by one machine and transferring them, through the keyboard, to the other. The adding machine produces typed numbers on a paper tape, but the typewriter only "understands" pressure on its keys. Hence, the operator not only carries the messages from the adding machine to the typewriter, but he also translates from one language to another.

It is uneconomical for a person to do a substantial amount of this transferring, translating, and copying when it can be done mechanically with more speed and accuracy. One solution to this problem is the punched-card machine, which approaches the problem of communications in the following way. The medium of communication in this type of system is a card on which one *column* is equivalent to one character of information. Holes punched in combinations of *rows* in a column represent these characters in a coded form in the same way as the dots and dashes in Morse code represent characters. Figure 1-7 shows a card with some codes punched in it.

By means of a beam of light that activates a photoelectric cell or brushes that make electrical contact through the holes punched in the card, punched-card machines can sense and "understand" the information punched in the card.

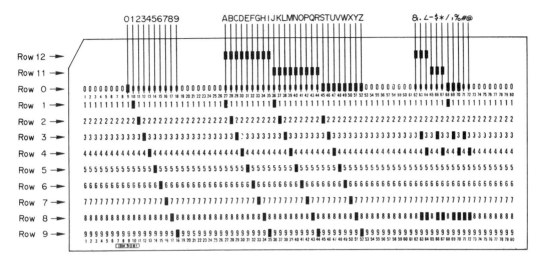

Figure 1-7   A punched card.

A punched card consists of 80 columns. Each column has 12 punching positions, or rows, which are named as indicated in Figure 1-7. Suppose the form of reading is by photocell. There are then 12 photocells lined up in a column, each photocell corresponding to one row of the card. The card is passed one column at a time over the photocells. Thus, the reading of the card could be considered to go on for 80 time frames, each frame corresponding to a column of the card being read. Thus, during time frame 27 column 27 is read, and assuming that the card shown in Figure 1-7 is being read, the photocells associated with rows 12 and 1 are activated. In this way the punched-card machine "knows" that an A is punched in column 27. A schematic of a photoelectric reading station is shown in Figure 1-8.

In an analogous fashion, punched-card machines can produce punched cards as output. In this case it is an initially *blank card* (a card with no holes punched in it) that is passed, one column at a time, over a set of 12 *punch dies* corresponding to the 12 card rows. During the 80 time frames during which the blank card is passed, the appropriate punch dies are activated to punch the code for a character in each of the 80 columns.

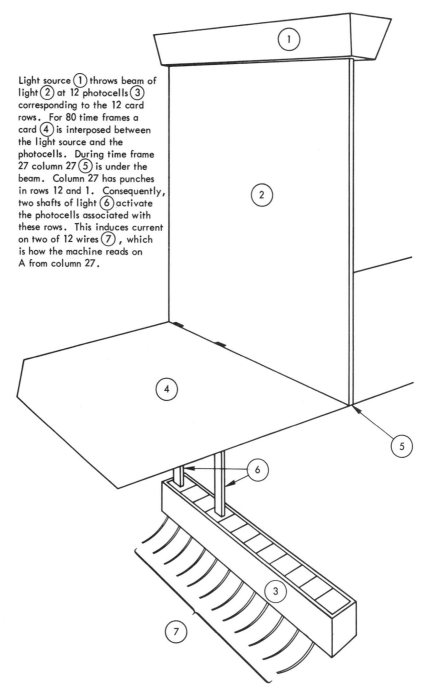

Light source ① throws beam of light ② at 12 photocells ③ corresponding to the 12 card rows. For 80 time frames a card ④ is interposed between the light source and the photocells. During time frame 27 column 27 ⑤ is under the beam. Column 27 has punches in rows 12 and 1. Consequently, two shafts of light ⑥ activate the photocells associated with these rows. This induces current on two of 12 wires ⑦ , which is how the machine reads on A from column 27.

Figure 1-8   Photoelectric reading station schematic.

Figure 1-9   Punching the inventory file into cards.

Thus, the machines "communicate" with each other through the medium of the holes in the punched card. All that is necessary is that, initially, all data to be processed must be punched into cards in the common or "machine language" code. These cards are then used by an array of specialized punched-card machines: sorters, collators, card reproducers, calculators, punches, and tabulators. Each of these machines performs one of the data-processing functions. As a consequence, punched-card machines are also "building block" machines and can be arranged in many ways to perform data-processing operations.

For example, the simplified inventory application might be done on punched-card equipment in the following way. Initially, the information in the inventory ledger has to be converted to punched-card form. This operation is executed on a keypunch, as shown in Figure 1-9.

A keypunch is a device similar to a typewriter. Both have a keyboard. A keystroke on a typewriter keyboard causes the character associated with the stroked key to be printed on a sheet of paper and then moves the paper one character position to the left in preparation for the typing of the next character. A keystroke on a keypunch keyboard causes the associated character to be punched in a card column and moves the card over one column in preparation for the punching of the next character. When a line has been typed on a typewriter, a carriage-return operation is performed to make the next line position available for typing. When a card has been punched in the keypunch, an eject operation is performed by depressing the eject key. This causes the card just punched to be *stacked* in a *stacker* (it is placed on the top of a pile of already punched cards in a receptacle designed for the purpose), and a blank card from the *hopper* (a feed bin filled with blank cards

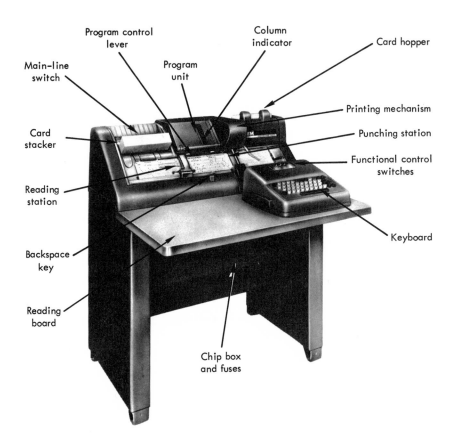

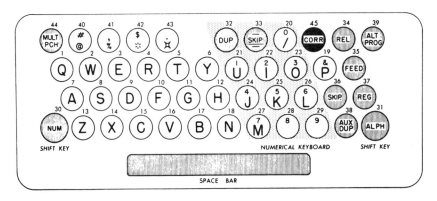

Figure 1-10 The card punch.

preparatory to the keypunching operation) is fed into the punch mechanism to become available for punching. The result of a typing operation is a typed sheet of paper. The result of a keypunching operation is a *deck* of punched cards that are removed from the stacker. A keypunch is pictured in Figure 1-10.

One card is produced for each commodity in the inventory. Each such card contains, in coded form, the stock number of the commodity that this card represents and the current inventory balance for this commodity. The cards in this deck are kept in stock number order, the same way the stock numbers were listed in the ledger.

Once prepared, this inventory card deck never has to be prepared again, because the punched-card system maintains the deck in much the same way as the clerk maintained the ledger.

When the sales slips are received from the sales organization, they are punched into cards, one card for each sales slip, on the keypunch. Each card in the sales deck now contains a stock number and a sales quantity. Another piece of card equipment called a *sorter* is then used to sort the cards into stock number order.

A sorter is a piece of punched-card equipment with one hopper and 13 stackers. Each stacker corresponds to a row that could be punched in the column of a card. (The thirteenth stacker is for a *blank column*, a column with no punches in it at all.) By means of a dial, the sorter operator selects the column on which the sorter is to sort. For example, suppose he selects column 17. Then the cards in the hopper are read one by one and stacked in the stacker corresponding to what is punched in column 17. (Such an operation is called a *pass* of the card deck.) Thus, if a card has a 3 punched in column 17, it would be stacked in the 3 stacker. A picture of a sorter is shown in Figure 1-11.

Consequently, if each card in the deck has only one punch in the column on which the sorting is done, the cards will be classified into 13 mutually exclusive piles at the end of the sort. However, if the column is *multipunched* (is punched in more than one row), a single sort pass will not achieve this result. Since in *Hollerith code* (the code of punch combinations that is commonly used to represent information in a punched card) numerics are represented by a single punch in a column and alphabetics by a multipunch, the sorter is a *numeric sorter* in operation, and a special, *multipass operation* must be used on it to sort alphabetics. This operation is not described here, but the procedure for sorting on a numeric key is described below.

Suppose the card deck is to be put into order on the basis of a key that appears in columns 1, 2, and 3 of each card. (This could

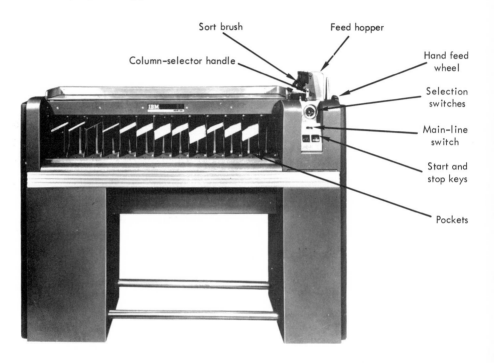

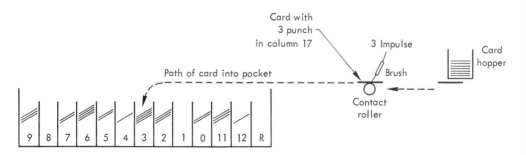

Figure 1-11   The sorter.

be the stock number in each card of the sales deck.) Also suppose that the following list of keys represents the cards as they appear in the deck in their original, unsorted order.

015
011
017
010
006
114
212
004
092
065
547

On the first pass of the cards through the sorter the sort is on column 3. The following deck order results.

010
011
212
092
114
004
015
065
006
017
547

On the second pass of the cards the sort is on column 2. The following deck order results.

004
006
010
011
212
114
015

017
547
065
092

On the third pass the sort is on column 1. The following deck order results.

004
006
010
011
015
017
065
092
114
212
547

The deck is now in order by stock number.

Now a piece of equipment called a collator is used. The collator has two input hoppers. The inventory card deck is placed in one of these hoppers; the sales deck is placed in the other. The collator also has a number of output stackers in which it stores cards that it has read. For the operation at hand, the collator is used to match the stock number of the inventory card in the bottom of the inventory deck hopper with the stock number of the sales card in the bottom of the sales deck hopper. If the stock numbers do not match, the inventory card is "not active" and is placed in one stacker. If the numbers match, the inventory card is active, and it, together with the sales card and all sales cards following having the same stock number, are placed in another ("active") stacker. This operation of the collator is shown schematically in Figure 1-12. A picture of a collator is shown in Figure 1-13.

As implied above, the collator is capable of performing a number of different operations, of which the *match merge* just described is only one. The operation to be performed is chosen by *wiring* the collator's *plugboard*. The plugboard is a removable, rectangular

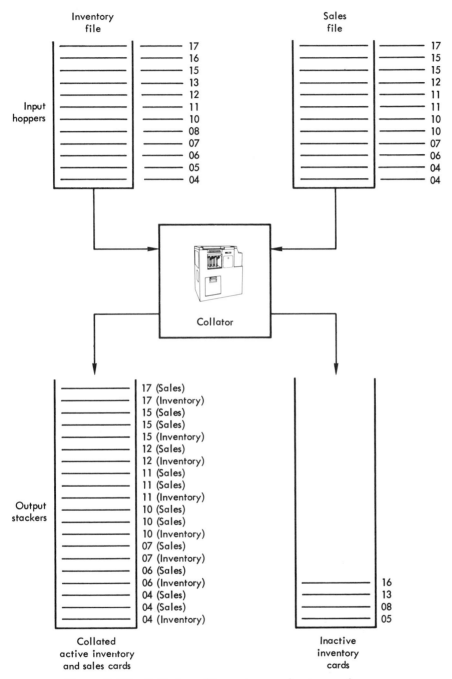

Figure 1-12 Collation of inventory and sales cards.

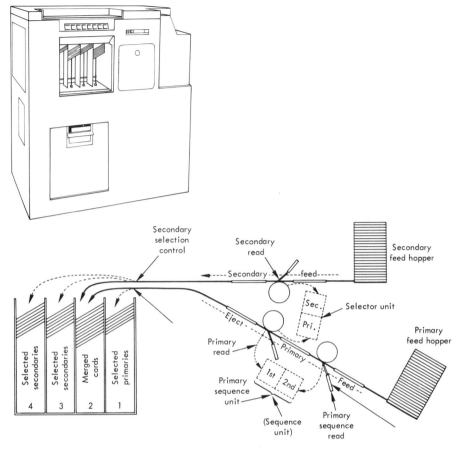

Figure 1-13 The collator.

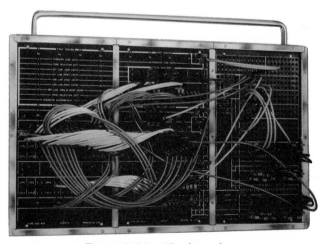

Figure 1-14 Plugboard.

board that fits into the collator. In the plugboard are a number of holes, called *hubs*. Thus, the board has an appearance similar to a honeycomb. A picture of a plugboard is shown in Figure 1-14.

The board is wired by means of *jumpers*, which are insulated wires with a pin on either end. One pin is placed in one hub and the other pin in another hub. The pins extend through the hubs to the other side of the board, as shown in Figure 1-15. When the board is seated into the collator, the extended pins make contact with the collator's circuitry. Thus, part of the collator's circuitry consists of the jumpers plugged into the board. By wiring the board in various ways, the collator's circuitry is modified, each modification causing it to perform a different function.

At the completion of the collation operation, the collated active inventory and sales cards are run through a tabulator, which subtracts the sales quantities in the sales cards from the on-hand quantities of the associated inventory cards.

Attached to the tabulator is an automatic card punch. For every active inventory card read into the tabulator, the punch produces from a blank card a new inventory card with the same stock number and the new on-hand amount supplied by the tabulator.

Finally, the collator is used once more. This time the updated inventory cards are placed in one input magazine and the previously inactive inventory cards are placed in the other. For this operation,

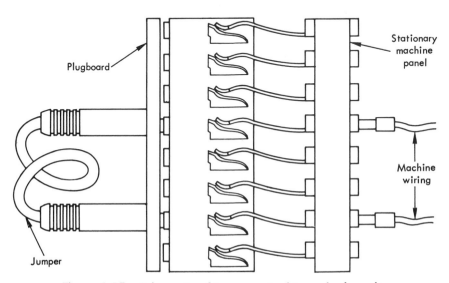

Figure 1-15 Schematic of jumper wired in a plugboard.

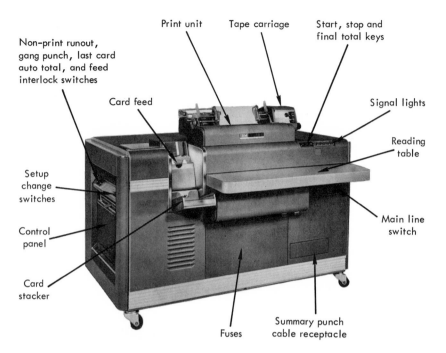

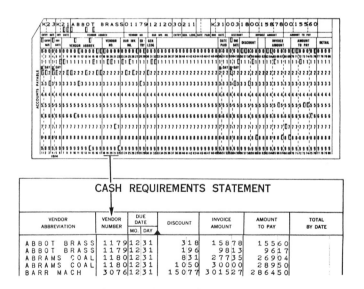

Figure 1-16 The tabulator.

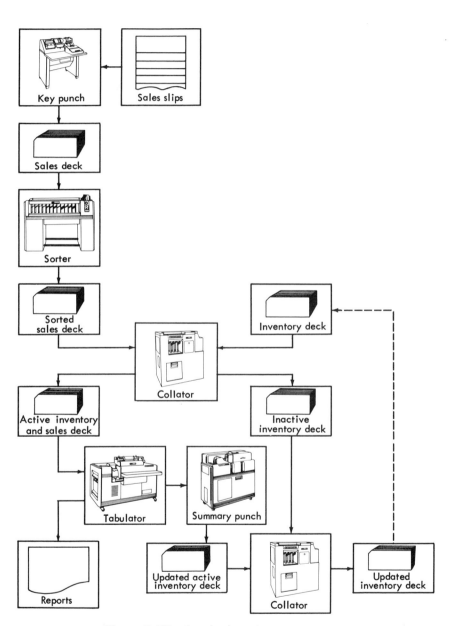

Figure 1-17   Punched card equipment.

the collator is wired to compare the stock number of the card at the bottom of the updated-inventory-card hopper with the stock number of the card at the bottom of the inactive-inventory-card hopper and place the one with the lower stock number in an output stacker. The collator then repeats this process over and over until all the cards are in stock number sequence in the stacker. This operation creates the updated inventory deck, which can be used as the inventory deck for the next day's operation.

Holes punched in cards are not conveniently read by people. Consequently, it is necessary in a punched-card installation to have some printing facility for preparing reports for management. This printing facility is located in the tabulator. In the case of the simplified inventory application, any necessary reports can be printed by the tabulator at the same time that it is updating the inventory balances.

The tabulator also contains a plugboard. By appropriate wiring of this board, the tabulator can be caused to do addition and subtraction on the values it reads from the cards that are put into it, to develop subtotals and totals, and to reformat this information for punching on cards and printing on paper. A picture of a tabulator is shown in Figure 1-16. A schematic of this system is shown in Figure 1-17.

The punched card also serves as a storage medium for information. In terms of the simplified inventory, this fact means that the inventory ledger has been replaced by the inventory card deck. The result of the communications and storage aspects of the punched card is that data processing becomes a materials-handling job. The punched cards are transferred from machine to machine and can be stored indefinitely for future use.

Other distinctions and similarities between a manual and a punched-card data-processing system are as follows.

1. The human illegibility of master files in punched-card form causes the report-creating aspect of a punched-card data-processing system to be more significant than in a manual system.
2. The fact that, at any particular time, only the bottom card in the input hopper is accessible to a punched-card machine

dictates that punched-card systems be sequential in nature. Thus, card deck sorting is a key feature of such systems.

3. Punched-card machines are designed to process decks of cards, not individual cards. This characteristic, plus the inability to do random processing and the continued problem of rapid routing of transactions to the data-processing center, militates against realtime processing. Punched-card systems are, by nature, batch data-processing systems.

4. The plugboard concept incorporated into punched-card equipment allows some amount of the procedure of a data-processing system to be built into the wiring of the board. However, punched-card equipment is still "building block" equipment, and a considerable amount of the procedure must still be carried out manually. The proper decks of information must still be fed into the proper machines in the proper sequence, and when using a machine, care must be taken to have the proper board mounted in it to obtain the desired result.

1-5 PUNCHED PAPER TAPE

Punched paper tape is another form of "machine language" medium. The approach here is the same as in punched cards: characters are represented in a coded form that consists of various combinations of punched holes. Paper tape could be considered to be a series of punched cards pasted together end-to-end. A card column corresponds to what is called a *frame* on paper tape. The row of a card corresponds to what is called a *channel*, as is shown in Figure 1-18.

The *sprocket channel* is used to feed the paper tape through the reader or punch. Paper tape may have five, six, seven, or eight channels, which are referred to respectively as five-, six-, seven-, and eight-*level* tape. Each level tape may have a different code of hole punching to represent characters, and some levels are used with more than one code.

Both card and paper-tape equipment read and punch cards (paper tape) a column (frame) at a time. However, the basic operating cycle of card equipment is to read (punch) a card, while that of paper-tape equipment is to read (punch) a frame. The read

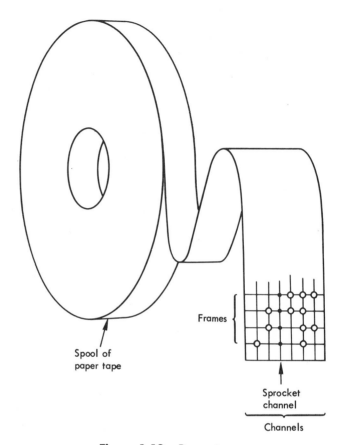

Figure 1-18 Paper tape.

(punch) structure of card equipment is fixed—when a read (punch) command is given, it is one card that is read (punched). When a read (punch) command is given on paper-tape equipment, the number of frames to be read (punched) is specified in some manner, and this specification is generally modifiable from command to command. Thus, each time card equipment reads (punches), it reads (punches) 80 columns. Paper-tape equipment may read (punch) 80 frames on one command, 40 frames on the next, and 120 on the third. As a consequence, record size on punched-card equipment is almost always 80 characters in length, corresponding to card size—the punched card is commonly referred to as a *unit record document.* There is no such restriction with respect to paper tape. Record size may be any number of characters that is convenient and may vary from record to record. It is for this reason that paper tape is used extensively in communications, where the major cost factor is the cost per character communicated. When used in this manner, the message is sent over wire and is punched out into paper tape on arrival at its destination.

However, the use of paper tape is not restricted to the field of communications. Paper-tape punches and readers can be attached to conventional office equipment such as typewriters or accounting machines with the result that information entered on the keyboard of these machines can be taken off in the form of punched paper tape. This resulting tape can be read by the same or other equipment. This reading of an already prepared tape allows the processing of information by the equipment without the necessity for reentering the information on the equipment keyboard.

There are various types of equipment that read paper tape and produce punched cards and vice versa. Therefore, paper-tape and punched-card equipment can be used cooperatively on the same batch of information without manually recording it in both paper-tape and punched-card form. One recording in either form is sufficient. For example, in the simplified inventory application, if the sales organization were geographically widespread, the sales slip information might be sent over wire and arrive in the accounting office in the form of paper tape. This paper-tape information can then be converted to punched cards, in which form it can enter the card system shown in Figure 1-17 at the point where the sales deck is sorted.

1-6
MAGNETIC TAPE

Besides punched cards and punched paper tape, a third type of bulk storage and communication medium is magnetic tape. Magnetic tape is similar to paper tape in that it comes in *spools* and is organized in terms of frames and channels. However, it differs in that, instead of being paper, the tape is plastic with a magnetizable coating. In this sense, it is similar to the tapes used on tape recorders.

Magnetic tape is read or written by means of tape handlers,

which also have many similarities to tape recorders. There are two *reels*, a *feed reel* and a *takeup reel*, and as the tape is passed from one reel to the other, it is passed over a *read-write head*. The read-write head has the ability to operate in either the read or the write mode. When in the write mode, the read-write head is capable of polarizing the magnetic surface of the magnetic tape at any intersection of a frame and channel, just as a paper-tape punch is capable of punching a hole in the paper tape at any intersection of a frame and channel. Thus, whereas the code in a paper-tape frame is a series of punches and no-punches in the paper-tape channels, the code in a magnetic-tape frame is a series of *magnetic spots* (polarized areas) or absences of magnetic spots in the magnetic-tape channels. Pictures of magnetic tape and a magnetic-tape handler are shown in Figure 1-19.

Information can be more densely packed (the frames can be put closer together) on magnetic tape than on paper tape. Also, magnetic tape can be moved at a higher rate of speed. These facts give magnetic tape its performance characteristics—more information stored in less space and a higher rate of reading and writing. They also result in another significant difference between paper and magnetic tape, described below.

Paper-tape equipment can stop paper-tape movement between any two frames of information. Recording density and operating speed makes such an operation impossible on magnetic tape. As a consequence, information recorded on magnetic tape is *blocked*. Information is recorded on the tape for some length (this is the *block* of information), and then there follows a length of tape with no information recorded on it (this is the *space between blocks*). Thus, information recorded on magnetic tape appears as an alternation of blocks and spaces between blocks. The tape handler reads or writes one block at a time, just as a card reader (punch) reads (punches) one card at a time. Consequently, between reads and writes, the read-write head is positioned in the middle of the space between blocks. When a read operation is performed, it is the space between blocks that is passing over the read-write head while the magnetic tape is getting up to speed. The block is then read, and it is once more a space-between-blocks area that is passing over the read-write head while the magnetic tape is being braked. It is this

Magnetic tape

0 1 2 3 4 5 6 7 8 9   A B C D E F G H I   J K L M N O P Q R   S T U V W X Y Z   & .   — $ * / , % # @

Check { C

Zone { B
        A

Numeric { 8
          4
          2
          1

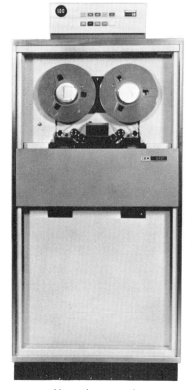

Magnetic tape unit

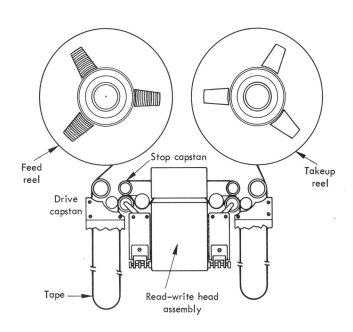

Feed reel

Stop capstan

Drive capstan

Takeup reel

Tape

Read—write head assembly

Figure 1-19   Magnetic tape.

speed pickup and braking action before and after a write operation that creates the space between blocks in the first place.

A tape handler can typically both read information from and write information on magnetic tape, and it can read the tape while it is moving in either the *forward* (feed reel to takeup reel) or *backward* (takeup reel to feed reel) direction. Also, once it has been *rewound* onto the feed reel, a spool of magnetic tape can be *dismounted* from a tape handler, and another spool can then be *mounted*.

Information is typically *blocked* on tape at some number of records, so that a block may consist of one, two, three, etc. number of records. Both the record and block size can be variable, so that the number of characters in a record or in a block can vary from record to record and from block to block. As in data-processsing systems utilizing punched cards, the human illegibility of information recorded on magnetic tape causes report creating to be a significant aspect of data-processing systems using magnetic tape as the bulk storage medium.

At any particular time, the only blocks on a magnetic tape that a tape handler can immediately read are the ones immediately to the right and to the left of its read-write head. To get at any other block, the tape handler must pass over the blocks that intervene between it and the read-write head. This fact constrains most data-processing systems using magnetic tape as the mass data storage medium to be sequential in nature. The fact that the tape handler can read backward as well as forward does give it some random data-processing characteristics, as it can move back and forth on the tape to randomly locate data. However, such operation is generally slow enough to be unacceptable. In addition, a tape handler does not have the capacity to selectively update a magnetic tape file. Its recording mechanism is imprecise enough so that the attempt to write over one block on tape may well damage the blocks surrounding the block overwritten. Therefore, updating a magnetic tape file requires that the file be *copied*, read on one tape handler, and written on another tape mounted on another tape handler. The information in the file is then updated at the time it is copied. It is this requirement to copy in order to update that dictates that data processing with magnetic-tape files be sequential in nature. The inability to do random processing also means that magnetic-tape data processing must be batch rather than realtime.

A common language medium in the form of punched cards and paper and magnetic tape is the third step in the evolution of data-processing systems. Except for data origination and the handling of bulk data (decks of cards and reels of tape), the human function in a common language data-processing system is reduced to following the right procedure. The following of such procedures is handled automatically by the computer, the latest step in the evolution of data-processing systems.

There are two basic differences between punched-card machines and computers. The first is that punched-card machines are "building block" machines. There is an array of special-purpose devices, each designed to do a specific function, such as sort, collate, print, and calculate. The computer is a general-purpose device. It has built into it the ability to perform the basic data-processing operations of input, arithmetic, logical decision, memory, control, and output, but it is not designed to do any specific data-processing function such as sort, collate, etc. The functions it is to perform depend on how it is *programmed.*

The other difference lies in the way punched-card machines and computers are programmed—that is, the way in which the procedure they are to follow is presented to them. Some punched-card machines, such as the sorter, are programmed by switches. Others, such as the collator, are programmed by plugboard. Computers, on the other hand, use the *stored program* concept. The computer is built to understand a limited number of commands such as

```
ADD A TO B
MOVE A TO B
SUBTRACT A FROM B
COMPARE A WITH B
```

and so on, where A and B can be specified by the *programmer.* The procedure the computer is to follow is written in terms of these commands or *instructions*. A procedure written in this language is called a *program*, and the man who writes such a program is known as a programmer. The program is then stored in the computer's memory, where the computer's control section accesses it and executes it.

The generality of the computer's construction plus the stored program concept are what allow the greater degree of procedure handling to be built into the computer's operation. For example, when using card equipment to handle the simplified inventory application, a collator pass followed by a tabulator pass followed by a second collator pass are required to apply the sorted sales file to the inventory file and produce an updated inventory file. All these operations can be combined into one automatic procedure on the computer.

1-7-1
Realtime
Computer Data
Processing

Computers may be used to do realtime or batch data processing. To do realtime data processing, the computer must be able to do random data processing. For example, to take the simplified inventory application as an illustration, if the computer is to reduce the on-hand quantity for any commodity at the time the commodity is sold and if any commodity in the line can be sold at any time, the computer must have relatively immediate access to the whole inventory file at all times. This need can be met by recording the inventory information on a *random access device*. Two examples of random access devices are *drums* and *disks*.

A drum can be conceived of as a cylinder with a number of rings of magnetic tape covering it (see Figure 1-20). These rings are called *tracks*. In reality, the tracks are not physical entities. The complete drum surface is magnetizable, and each track is recorded in a fixed place on the surface.

On some drums there is a read-write head for each track as shown in Figure 1-20. As in the case of magnetic tape, information on drum tracks is blocked, although in random access devices the blocks are commonly referred to as *sectors*. Unlike magnetic tape, on which block location is somewhat variable, the location of a sector on a drum track is precisely fixed. Thus, any sector on the

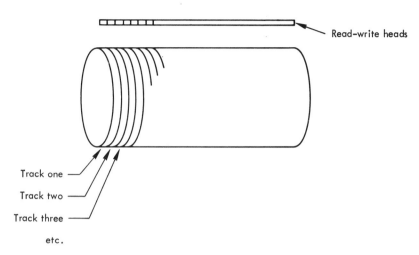

Track one

Track two

Track three

etc.

Figure 1-20   Drum schematic.

drum can be *addressed* in terms of the track on which it lies and its location on the track.

The drum revolves under the read-write heads. When the computer wishes to read a sector into its memory, it sends the sector's *address* to the drum unit. The drum unit selects the appropriate track and then waits until the appropriate sector begins to pass under the read-write head, at which time it reads the information from the sector into the computer's memory. Similarly, when the computer desires to write information in a particular sector area, it sends the sector address to the drum unit, which waits until the appropriate area is passing under the appropriate read-write head, at which point it reads from the computer's memory the information to be written and writes this information into the sector area of the drum. The time during a read or a write that the computer is waiting for the appropriate sector to pass under the read-write head is called *latency time*.

Not all drums have a read-write head for every track. For example, there might be a read-write head for every third track. Such read-write heads are mounted on a bar, and the bar is moved to position a read-write head over the track from (on) which it is desired to read (write), as shown schematically in Figure 1-21. Consequently, unless a read-write head is already positioned over the appropriate track when a read or write command is given, an arm-positioning operation must be performed before the search for the appropriate sector can begin. The time required to do this arm positioning is called *access time.*

A disk is a platter similar to a conventional home music record except that there is not one spiral track but instead a number of concentric circular tracks, each one of which is analogous to a drum track in that each disk track has a number of sectors recorded on it in fixed locations. A disk unit typically has a single read-write head associated with it. This read-write head is mounted on the end of an arm in a fashion similar to the needle of a phonograph turntable arm. The disk rotates as does a record. When it is desired to read (write) a sector from (onto) a disk sector, the arm is moved until the read-write head is positioned over the appropriate track, at which point the disk unit waits until the appropriate sector begins to pass under the read-write head. Thus, reading and writing on a disk also involve access and latency time.

A fundamental difference between drums and disks is that disks can generally be mounted and dismounted from the disk unit in a fashion similar to the way in which magnetic tape reels are

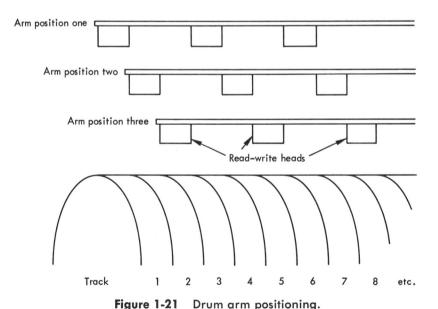

Figure 1-21 Drum arm positioning.

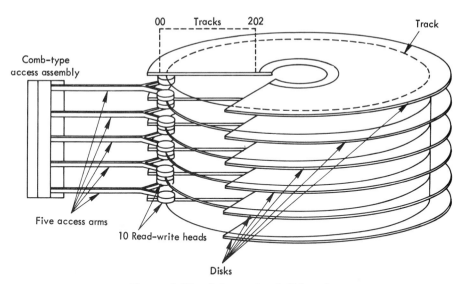

Figure 1-22   Schematic of disk unit.

mounted and dismounted from a tape handler, while a drum is an integral part of a drum unit and cannot, as a normal operating procedure, be removed. A schematic of a disk unit is shown in Figure 1-22. This disk unit allows for the mounting of a package of several disks at once. Such a package is referred to as a *cartridge*. The disk unit has an access arm equipped with a read-write head for each surface of each disk. In such an arrangement, a sector is addressed by disk surface, track on the selected disk surface, and sector on the selected track.

A second item the computer requires to handle the simplified inventory application is some mechanism to allow each transaction to be entered into the computer for processing as it occurs. This requirement can be met by some type of keyboard device that allows the salesman to send the necessary information to the computer at the same time he is recording the sale for the customer.

The way in which such a computer updates the inventory on the basis of a sale is as follows. At the time of the sale, the salesman keys into his keyboard device the stock number and quantity-sold information. At this point this information remains stored in the device and generally is also displayed in some manner. When the salesman has convinced himself that he has keyed in the correct information, he depresses a *release key* on the console of his keyboard device. Depression of the release key does two things.

1. It causes an *interrupt* in the computer, which tells the computer that a sales transaction record is being transmitted from one of the remote keyboard devices. It also tells the computer from which device the information is being transmitted.

2. Depression of the release key also causes the information previously keyed into the device to be sent out on the line that connects the device with the computer.

As a result, the computer is prepared to read into its memory the sales record being transmitted from the remote device.

Once the sales record has been read in this manner, the computer knows what the stock number of the commodity sold is. On the basis of this information, the computer locates the master inventory record with the matching stock number on the random access device and reads this master record into memory. The master record is generally located by means of some relationship between the key of the record and the address of the sector in which it is stored.

After reading the master record, the computer has the on-hand quantity stored in memory. It reduces this quantity by the quantity sold, which updates the master record in memory. The computer then writes this updated master record from memory onto its sector on the random access device, which brings the inventory up to date. The computer then waits for the next interrupt to occur.

In the above description, the computer interrupt is a feature of the computer hardware. All other operations involved in updating the inventory are done in response to the execution of instructions stored in the computer's memory. These instructions make up the program that was expressly written to cause the computer to update the inventory.

The updating of the inventory is not instantaneous. The keying of the sales information, its transmission to the computer, the execution of the computer's program, the reading and writing of the inventory record, and the access and latency time required all take time. However, as long as the total of this transaction handling time

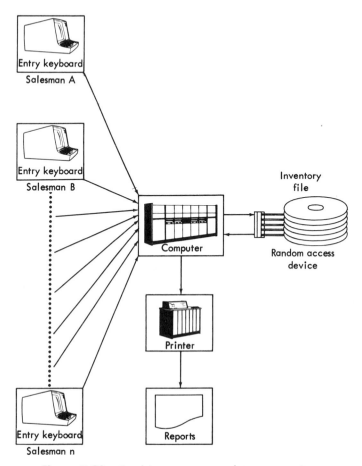

Figure 1-23   Realtime computer data processing.

is somewhat less than the mean time between sales, the computer can keep up with the sales activity, and in this sense the application is realtime.

Finally, since all inventory information is stored on the random access device and is not accessible to management, a printer must be available to the computer so all required reports can be printed. A schematic of the realtime computer system described above is shown in Figure 1-23.

The advantage of the realtime computer is that the application in which it is used involves master data that is up-to-date. For example, in the simplified inventory application, the inventory data reflects the current inventory situation. However, if the computer is to apply transaction data randomly to the master data as the transaction data occurs, all the master data must always be stored on the random access device. For example, in the inventory application, the inventory data must always be stored on the random access device. This fact has a tendency to limit the uses to which the computer can be put.

1-7-2
Batch Computer Data Processing

When a computer is being used to do batch data processing, the master data is typically not stored on a random access device but rather on some sequential access medium such as punched-card decks or magnetic tape. Consequently, addition of more applications with various master files to the computer data-processing system is a matter of recording the master files involved. A consequence of this approach is that no master file is available to the computer in its entirety. Therefore, transaction data cannot be applied as it occurs. Instead, transaction data is batched over a period of time and is applied by the computer to the master data in the resulting batches on a cyclical basis. This approach results in no master file ever being completely up-to-date. However, the speed and accuracy with which the computer operates allows a cyclical updating period of short duration.

As an example of a batch computer operation, consider the simplified inventory application as it might be applied to a batch computer equipped with the facility for handling magnetic tape files.

When the computer is first introduced as the data processor, the inventory tape would have to be prepared in some way. For example, it might be punched into cards, the punched-card deck then being converted to tape as shown in Figure 1-24.

The card-to-tape conversion shown in Figure 1-24 is accomplished in the following way. The computer on which the conversion is to be done must be equipped with a card reader and at least one magnetic tape handler. (Computers on which data processing is going to be essentially tape oriented generally are equipped with at least four magnetic-tape handlers.) The card-to-tape conversion

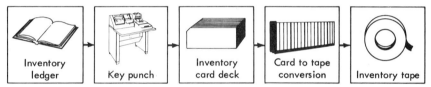

Figure 1-24   Converting the inventory file to magnetic tape.

program is loaded into memory. This loading can be done either from the card reader or a tape handler. The inventory card deck is then placed in the card reader, and a *blank tape* is mounted on the tape handler. (A blank tape is usually not "blank" in the sense that there is no information recorded on it. It is blank in the sense that whatever is on it is of no use anymore and consequently can be overwritten.)

Execution of the card-to-tape conversion program then begins. The computer reads the first card from the card read unit into its memory. It then writes the information, read from the card, from its memory onto the magnetic tape. It then reads the second card and writes the information onto tape. Then the third card. This continues until there are no more cards to read. The card-to-tape conversion is then complete. Once prepared, this inventory tape never has to be prepared again, because the computer maintains it in much the same way as the punched-card system maintained the information in punched-card form.

The company operation generates the sales slips for the computer system the same way as before. These sales slips are key-punched, one punched card for each sales slip, in the same way they were in the punched-card system, so that they can be read by the computer. The computer then reads these cards one at a time and sorts these sales records into stock number order. This card-to-tape conversion and sort are also done by program. The basic structure of this program is as follows.

At the beginning of program execution, the situation is as shown in Figure 1-25. In this figure, each card in the input hopper of the card read unit is represented by its key. Four tape units, numbered 1, 2, 3, and 4, are also required. Blank tapes are mounted on these tape units.

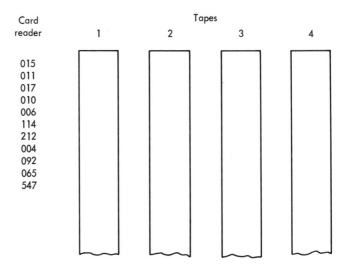

Figure 1-25 Situation at the beginning of the sort.

The computer reads the sales records one by one from the card read unit and writes them alternately on tape units 1 and 2. Thus, the sales record with the key of 015 is written on tape unit 1, the sales record with the key of 011 on tape unit 2, the sales record

Card reader	Tapes 1	2	3	4
015	015	011		
011	017	010		
017	006	114		
010	212	004		
006	092	065		
114	547			
212				
004				
092				
065				
547				

Figure 1-26 Situation at the end of the dispersion pass.

with the key of 017 on unit 1, and so on, until the situation shown in Figure 1-26 is created.

This initial pass of the sort is called the *dispersion pass*. At the end of the dispersion pass, tapes 1 and 2 are rewound, and the first record from each is read into memory. These two records are written on tape 3, the one with the smaller key being written before the one with the larger. The second record from tape 1 and the second record from tape 2 are then read into memory, and these two records are written on tape 4, the one with the smaller key being written first. The third record from tape 1 and the third record from tape 2 are *merged* together and written on tape 3. This continues, pairs of records being merged together and the pairs being written alternately on tapes 3 and 4 until the situation shown in Figure 1-27 is created.

The second pass of the sort is called the *first collation pass*. During the first collation pass pairs of records that are in order have been written on tapes 3 and 4. These pairs are called *strings* and are separated in Figure 1-27 by lines drawn on the representation of tapes 3 and 4.

At the end of the first collation pass, all four tapes are rewound. The first record from tape 3 and the first record from tape 4 are read into memory. The record with the smaller key is written on tape 1. This is the record with key 010, which came from tape 4. The next record from tape 4 is then read into memory. Of the two records now in memory, the one with the smaller key is written on tape 1. This is the record with key 011, which came from tape 3. The next record from tape 3 is then read into memory. The two records now in memory are then written on tape 1, the one with the smaller key being written first. This completes the merge of the first two-record string from tape 3 with the first two-record string from tape 4 into one four-record string on tape 1.

The second two-record string from tape 3 and the second two-record string from tape 4 are then merged to produce a four-record string on tape 2. Finally, the third string from tape 3 and the third string from tape 4 are merged into one string and written on tape 1. The situation shown in Figure 1-28 has then been created. This pass of the sort is called the *second collation pass*.

At the end of the second collation pass, all four tapes are

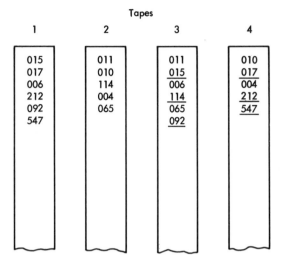

Tapes

1	2	3	4
015	011	011	010
017	010	015	017
006	114	006	004
212	004	114	212
092	065	065	547
547		092	

Figure 1-27   Situation at the end of the first collation pass.

rewound. The first string from tape 1 and the first string from tape 2 are then merged into one string and written on tape 3. The second string from tape 1 is then copied onto tape 4 to produce the situation shown in Figure 1-29. At the end of this *third collation pass*, all

Tapes

1	2	3	4
010	004	011	010
011	006	015	017
015	114	006	004
017	212	114	212
065		065	547
092		092	
547			

Figure 1-28   Situation at the end of the second collation pass.

Tapes

1	2	3	4
010	004	004	065
011	006	006	092
015	114	010	<u>547</u>
<u>017</u>	<u>212</u>	011	
065		015	
092		017	
<u>547</u>		114	
		<u>212</u>	

Figure 1-29   Situation at the end of the third collation pass.

four tapes are rewound. The two strings on tapes 3 and 4 are then merged to produce the sorted sales file on tape 1, as shown in Figure 1-30.

Many refinements to improve sorting efficiency are present in tape sorts used today, but they all embody the same basic structure.

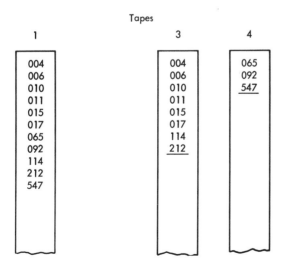

Tapes

1	3	4
004	004	065
006	006	092
010	010	<u>547</u>
011	011	
015	015	
017	017	
065	114	
092	<u>212</u>	
114		
212		
547		

Figure 1-30   Situation at the end of the last collation pass.

1. An initial pass during which the records to be sorted are dispersed over at least two tapes.
2. A series of collation passes during which strings are merged to produce larger strings until, in the *last collation pass*, the the sort output is produced.

The sorted sales tape is then applied by the computer to the inventory tape to produce an updated inventory tape. This update program has the following structure. The updated inventory tape is a reproduction of the current inventory tape except that those changes in stock level required by the information on the sales tape have been made. The program to produce the updated inventory tape is described in more detail below.

The current inventory tape is mounted on one tape handler, the sorted sales tape is mounted on a second handler, and a blank is mounted on a third handler. It is on this blank tape that the updated inventory file is to be written.

The first inventory record and the first sales record are read from their respective files into the computer's memory. The stock number field of the inventory record currently in the memory is then compared with the stock number field of the current sales record. If the two stock numbers are not equal, the current inventory record is not altered but instead becomes the current updated inventory record, which is recorded on the blank tape (the updated inventory file); the next inventory record is read from the inventory file into the memory; and the comparison of stock numbers is once more made. As long as this comparison does not check out for equality, this process continues, since the arrangement of the records in the files determines that the current sales record refers to an inventory record that is further down the inventory file and that all records preceding this inventory record on the inventory file were not active during the period in which the current sales file was being compiled. When the stock numbers of the current inventory and sales records prove to be equal, the quantity-on-hand field of the current inventory record is reduced by the quantity-sold field of the current sales record, the next sales record from the sales tape is read, and the comparison of stock numbers is resumed. Notice that the inventory record just updated does not immediately become the updated inventory record, since more than one sales record may refer to it. This process is continued until there are no more sales records, at which point there are no more inventory records to be updated and the inventory records remaining on the inventory file are moved to the updated inventory file. When there are no more inventory records, the run is complete.

A more formal statement of this logical analysis is shown below.

1. Read the first inventory record.
2. Read the first sales record.
3. Compare the stock number field of the current inventory record with the stock number field of the current sales record. If they are equal, go to step 8.
4. Make the current inventory record the current updated inventory record.
5. Write the current updated inventory record.
6. Read the next inventory record. If there are no more, go to step 13.
7. Go to step 3.
8. Subtract the quantity-sold field of the current sales record from the quantity-on-hand field of the current inventory record.
9. Read the next sales record. If there are no more, go to step 11.
10. Go to step 3.
11. Change step 7 to go to step 4.
12. Go to step 4.
13. Stop.

The updated inventory tape produced on one day becomes the inventory input tape on the next day, whereas the sales tape continues to originate from without the system.

In any data-processing system, it becomes necessary from time to time to inspect the results of the processing. Thus, for example, in the manual inventory system previously described, management will want to see the stock levels for various stock items. Although many of the purposes for which management would want to make

Figure 1-31   Batch computer data processing.

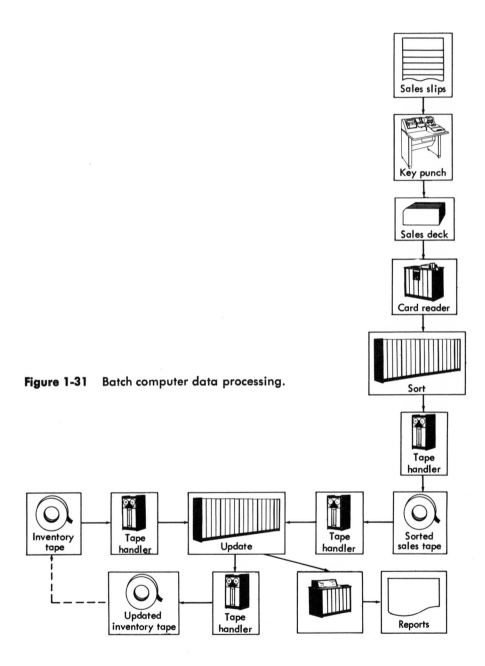

this inspection will be handled automatically by the computer, with the result that manual reference to the files in a computer system should be less than such reference in any other kind of system, there will be occasions when it will be necessary for management to view the records maintained by the computer. Since a tape record is neither visible nor legible, it is necessary in a computer system to have some type of printing equipment to produce the reports required by management. The computer can then print the information to appear in the report during the updating of the inventory file. A schematic of this computer system is shown in Figure 1-31.

EXERCISES

Design the part of an accounts-receivable system that posts payments to outstanding accounts. Design the system for:

1. Manual data processing;
2. Punched-card data processing;
3. Sequential magnetic-tape oriented data processing;
4. Realtime data processing.

2 REPRESENTATION OF INFORMATION

2-1 GRAPHICS

The thing a computer processes is information. This information must be intelligible to the computer. The computer must also be capable of communicating this information to us, its users.

A computer may communicate information to us by printing it on a printer. Thus, information is represented by strings of printed characters, or *graphics*. The extent to which a computer can communicate information in a printed form depends on its graphic set. A common number of characters in a graphic set is 64. One possible set is as follows.

1. The 26 alphabetics, A through Z
2. The ten numerics, 0 through 9
3. Twenty-seven special graphics, such as ampersand, minus sign, slash, cent sign, exclamation point, colon, period, dollar sign, comma, number sign, less than symbol, asterisk, percent sign, at sign, left parenthesis, right parenthesis, apostrophe, plus sign, semicolon, greater than symbol, and question mark

4. The space symbol, sometimes represented in texts as ƀ, but always standing for a blank space one graphic wide

2-2
CARD CODE

One way in which a computer handles information is in card code. It reads information having previously been punched into cards, and it records information for future use by punching it into cards. To be intelligible, information must be punched into the cards in a standard code, the Hollerith code. Hollerith code has the following structure.

A punched card, shown in Figure 1-7, is made up of 80 columns. In general, one character of information is punched into one column. Each column has 12 punching positions, or rows, which are named as indicated in Figure 1-7. The 12 and 11 rows are sometimes referred to as *overpunch* rows, although a punch in the zero row is also often used as an overpunch.

2-2-1
Representating Numerics

The numbers 0 through 9 are represented in Hollerith code by a single punch in the row corresponding to the number. For example, the numbers 0 through 9 are shown in Figure 1-7 punched in columns 9 through 18, respectively. For this reason, rows 0 through 9 of the card are called the *digit portion* of the card, and rows 12 and 11 are called the overpunch or *zone portion* of the card. In a field of columns containing numeric data only, leading zeros are sometimes conventionally represented by blank columns as well as by zero-punched columns.

2-2-2
Representing Alphabetics

The alphabetics, A through Z, and all special characters are represented by *multiple punches* in a column. The multiple punching for all alphabetics is a double punch and follows a pattern. A through I are represented by a 12 overpunch together with a 1 through 9 digit punch, respectively. J through R are represented by an 11 overpunch together with a 1 through 9 digit punch. S through Z are represented by a zero overpunch together with a 2 through 9 punch. For example, the alphabetics A through Z are shown in Figure 1-7 in columns 27 through 52, respectively.

2-2-3
Representing Special Characters

Special characters are also represented by multiple punches. Some special characters are shown punched in columns 67 through 72 of the card in Figure 1-7. A more complete listing of Hollerith code for special characters is given in Table 2-1.

Table 2-1

Character	Code
Ampersand (&)	12
Minus sign (—)	11
Slash (/)	0–1
Cent sign (¢)	12–8–2
Exclamation point (!)	11–8–2
Colon (:)	8–2
Period (.)	12–8–3
Dollar sign ($)	11–8–3
Comma (,)	0–8–3
Number sign (#)	8–3
Less than symbol (<)	12–8–4
Asterisk (*)	11–8–4
Percent sign (%)	0–8–4
At sign (@)	8–4
Left parenthesis [(]	12–8–5
Right parenthesis [)]	11–8–5
Apostrophe (')	8–5
Plus sign (+)	12–8–6
Semicolon (;)	11–8–6
Greater than symbol (>)	0–8–6
Equal symbol (=)	8–6
Question mark (?)	0–8–7

2-2-4
Representing Sign Quantities

The sign of a numeric field is conventionally represented as an overpunch of the least significant column of the field. No overpunch or a 12 overpunch causes the contents of the field to be treated as

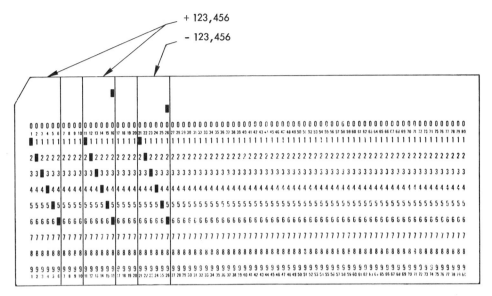

Figure 2-1   Examples of positive and negative quantities.

a positive quantity, an 11 overpunch as a negative quantity. Thus, in Figure 2-1 columns 1 through 6 and columns 11 through 16 both contain the positive quantity 123,456; columns 21 through 26, the negative quantity −123,456.

2-2-5
Other Uses of Overpunching

Since the zone portion of all columns of a numeric field but the least significant is never used in the representation of the numeric quantity, it is often used to represent other information. Thus, if an employee's Social Security number is punched in columns 53 through 61 of a card, the employee's sex can be represented in the zone portion of column 53. For example, no overpunch could indicate a male employee and an 11 overpunch a female employee.

2-3
INTERNAL REPRESENTATION

A number of techniques are used to represent information internally in a computer—voltage levels on a line, presence or absence of magnetic spots, polarity of magnets, etc. All of these techniques lend themselves most readily to a two-stable-state representation. This is like the light in your bedroom—it has two states, on and off, and once put in one of its states, it is stable. A definite action (the throwing of the light switch) is required to change the state. Two-stable-state devices lend themselves most readily to a *binary* representation of information.

2-3-1
Internal
Representation

Any positive number can be represented by a row of marks, such as 111111111 (or 9), although all but the smallest numbers become unwieldy in such notation. For ease of manipulation a *positional notation* using symbols to represent different rows of marks is more convenient. One such notation is the *Arabic*, which uses ten different symbols or digits: 0, 1, 2, 3, 4, 5, 6, 7, 8, and 9.

The number of different digits used in a positional notation or system is known as the *base* of the system. Using one digit position, quantities as large as nine can be represented in the *decimal* system. To represent a quantity larger than nine another digit position must be used. Thus, to represent the quantity ten a carry is made into the digit position to the left, and the original digit position reverts to zero. The expansion of this system is exemplified by the odometer of a car. In positional notation each digit position, or column, implies a power of the base as a multiplier of the digit in the column. The decimal number 1076 is positional notation for the expression

$$(1 \times 1000) + (0 \times 100) + (7 \times 10) + (6 \times 1)$$

The columns imply powers of ten

$$
\begin{aligned}
1 &= 1 & &= 10^0 \\
10 &= 10 & &= 10^1 \\
100 &= 10 \times 10 & &= 10^2 \\
1000 &= 10 \times 10 \times 10 &= 10^3
\end{aligned}
$$

and are named the units column, the tens column, the hundreds column, and so on.

The binary system can be built up in a way analogous to the decimal. There are two possible digits, 0 and 1, used in conjunction with successive powers of two.

$$
\begin{aligned}
2^0 &= 1 \\
2^1 &= 2
\end{aligned}
$$

$$2^2 = 4$$
$$2^3 = 8$$

. .

. .

. .

Thus, the binary equivalent of a decimal nine is 1001, which is binary notation for the expression

$$(1 \times 8) + (0 \times 4) + (0 \times 2) + (1 \times 1)$$

Table 2-2 shows the binary equivalents of the ten decimal digits.

Table 2-2

	Decimal	Binary 8421
	0	0000
	1	0001
	2	0010
	3	0011
	4	0100
	5	0101
	6	0110
	7	0111
	8	1000
	9	1001

Each digit of a binary number is called a *bit* (from *bi*nary dig*it*).

2-3-2
Binary Coded Decimal Representation

For decimally oriented people like ourselves, the handling of binary numbers of all but the smallest in magnitude is unwieldy. For example, the binary equivalent of a decimal 1000 is 1111101000. As a result, a compromise is generally struck between the computer designer's inclination toward binary notation and the user's desire for decimal. The compromise is *binary coded decimal* representation. In this representation, only the binary equivalents of the ten decimal digits are used as a code for the decimal digits. Any decimal number greater than nine is represented by a combination of these codes. For example, the decimal number 147 would be represented as

0001   0100   0111

A binary representation consisting of four bits is sufficient to provide distinct codes for all ten decimal digits. However, a listing of all possible combinations of ones and zeros in a four-bit representation demonstrates that the representation is capable of supplying codes for only 16 different things.

1	0001
2	0010
3	0011
4	0100
5	0101
6	0110
7	0111
8	1000
9	1001
10	1010
11	1011
12	1100
13	1101
14	1110
15	1111
16	0000

In a computer in which we wish to represent the ten decimal digits, the 26 alphanumeric characters, and several special characters, a four-bit representation is not sufficient for our needs. It is necessary to extend the representation to include a larger number of bits. One such extension is the *Extended Binary Coded Decimal Interchange Code* (EBCDIC), in which the code representation is extended to eight bits. The extension is analogous to Hollerith code

Table 2-3

Character	EBCDIC		Hollerith Code	
	Zone	*Numeric*	*Zone*	*Numeric*
0	1111	0000	—	0
1	1111	0001	—	1
2	1111	0010	—	2
3	1111	0011	—	3
4	1111	0100	—	4
5	1111	0101	—	5
6	1111	0110	—	6
7	1111	0111	—	7
8	1111	1000	—	8
9	1111	1001	—	9
A	1100	0001	12	1
B	1100	0010	12	2
C	1100	0011	12	3
D	1100	0100	12	4
E	1100	0101	12	5
F	1100	0110	12	6
G	1100	0111	12	7
H	1100	1000	12	8
I	1100	1001	12	9
J	1101	0001	11	1
K	1101	0010	11	2
L	1101	0011	11	3
M	1101	0100	11	4
N	1101	0101	11	5
O	1101	0110	11	6
P	1101	0111	11	7
Q	1101	1000	11	8
R	1101	1001	11	9
S	1110	0010	0	2
T	1110	0011	0	3
U	1110	0100	0	4
V	1110	0101	0	5
W	1110	0110	0	6
X	1110	0111	0	7
Y	1110	1000	0	8
Z	1110	1001	0	9

in that the four least significant bits of the representation retain the characteristic of representing the ten decimal digits in BCD, whereas the four most significant bits are used as a zone added onto the basic BCD representation. The analogy to a digit punch extended by overpunching is emphasized in Table 2-3, which shows the EBCDIC and Hollerith code for the ten digits and 26 alphabetics. When it is considered that EBCDIC treats the zone of the least significant digit of a number as the number's sign, that zones of 1111 and 1100 are treated as plus signs (no overpunch and 12 overpunch), and that 1101 is treated as a minus sign (11 overpunch), the analogy is complete.

Even though zones of 1111 and 1100 are both treated as plus signs, when an arithmetic operation is performed and the result is positive a zone of 1100 is supplied to represent the plus sign.

EXERCISES

1. What are graphics?

2. What is the digit portion of a punched card? The zone portion?

3. How are numbers represented in a punched card? Alphabetics?

4. How is the sign carried on a punched card?

5. Take a punched card and represent the following on it:

    +14627
    −53
    CHARLIE

6. Show how the following numbers are represented in binary coded decimal:

    63
    127
    4

7. How are numbers represented in EBCDIC? Alphabetics?

3 INTRODUCTION TO PROGRAMMING

Programming is the preparation of a series of instructions to direct a computer in the execution of a task. The task may be the solution of a set of mathematical equations, the preparation of a payroll, or the updating of an inventory. Ideally these directions to the computer would be expressed directly in the user's language. Unfortunately, this ideal situation does not exist. The internal operation of a computer is controlled by electrical impulses that must be coded in some way to bridge the gap between the user's language and the electronic functions that comprise the computer.

There are certain economic and physical considerations in the structure of a computer that limit the nature of the coding and therefore restrict the nature of the language that can be used to communicate with the computer. For example, to represent the decimal number system directly in the computer without resorting to some form of coding, each electrical pulse would have to be capable of ten variations. A computer constructed to handle such pulses would be uneconomical because of the amount of circuitry required to keep the pulse variations separate and stable.

A reliable and effective way to represent data within a computer is suggested by the fundamental electronic operation of switching: on/off, current/no current, voltage/no voltage, and so forth. This approach reduces the number of required variations from ten to two, and it is less expensive to construct a circuit that will respond to the presence or absence of a pulse than one that responds to ten discrete variations of a pulse. A system in which only two values are permitted can handle any kind of decimal or alphabetic data, but to do so, a coded system of representation is required. Thus, if the two values the computer can handle are represented by 0 and 1, codes for the decimal numbers 0 through 9 might be 0000, 0001, 0010, 0011, 0100, 0101, 0110, 0111, 1000, and 1001. This system of representation is binary, and it is the internal language of most digital computers.

Apart from the language difference, which erects a fundamental barrier to easy communication between man and computers, a computer must also be carefully directed through every step of its operation. For example, the question $2 + 2 =?$ cannot be expressed to a computer in this way. The request must be more detailed; it must be a series of explicit directions, or *instructions*.

To describe the nature of these instructions, a more detailed understanding of some features of the computer's construction must be given.

1. The computer's memory is divided up into a number of cells, or *memory locations*. Each memory location can contain a fixed amount of information. Each location also has a unique name, or *address*, by which it is identified. The locations are generally numbered in sequence, so there is a memory location 0, a location 1, location 2, and so on, for as many locations as comprise the memory.

2. For reasons of economy, computers are typically supplied with *registers*, and before arithmetic operations are performed on values, the values are transferred to registers from the memory locations in which they are stored. Registers also have the capacity to store a fixed amount of information, and they are also assigned identifying addresses.

With the above information, it is now possible to describe the series of instructions that might have to be written to direct the computer to answer the question $2 + 2 = ?$

1. Go to memory location X and transfer the contents found there to register A.
2. Go to memory location Y and add the contents found there to register A.
3. Transfer the contents of register A to memory location Z.
4. Print out the contents of memory location Z.

A complete statement of the directions to answer the question $2 + 2 = ?$ would also include instructions for storing the values to be added in locations X and Y.

Once a problem is stated explicitly, it must then be converted into the binary language of the computer before it is meaningful to the computer. For example, instruction 2 in the preceding paragraph, "Go to memory location Y and add the contents found there to register A," may look like this in the computer:

$$01010101100000000000100111100111$$

Communication with a computer is thus a tedious process of carefully describing in complete detail all the steps that the computer must follow to perform a task and then translating these steps into a language in which all words are spelled with only two letters. This procedure must be performed faultlessly, or the result of the computer operation will be incorrect.

In summary, the computer user would like to express the operations he wants performed in the rich, generalized language with which he is familiar, but economic considerations in the manufacture of computers rule out this form of expression and require instead that instructions be spelled out in considerable detail in a coded form.

Fortunately, the computer itself can be used to handle the problem of conversion between languages. A body of programs, called *language processors*, has been developed whose purpose is to accept as input an operation described in the user's language and to produce as output that same operation described in the language of the computer. The input to the language processor is *source code*;

the output is *object code*. The object code can then be used to direct the operation of the computer.

One such language processer is the Report Program Generator (RPG). The source language of the RPG is divided into three parts: input, calculation, and output. There is a form for each part. On the input form the user describes the input to the run he wishes to program. The input is described in terms of files, the different record types present in each file, and the fields of data in each record type. The user assigns each field a name and describes it in terms of in which record it is found, its location in the record, its length, whether it is numeric or alphanumeric, and if it is numeric, where its decimal point is located. On the output form the user describes the format of the run output. This description is also in terms of files, records, fields, assigned names, and field characteristics. On the calculation form the user describes any calculations that are to be done on the input fields to produce output fields. The RPG produces from this source language an object program that will read the input described, do the specified calculations, and produce the output specified.

EXERCISE

Draw a diagram representing the relation between source code, object code, and a language processor.

4 INTRODUCTION TO THE RPG

The object program generated by the RPG has a basic processing cycle from which it never varies. This cycle is shown in Figure 4-1.

To see how this cycle is used, suppose we have a deck of cards in which information is punched in Hollerith code. Suppose further we would like to see what is punched in these cards. What we need for this purpose is a listing of the cards. This is a printed report in which each card is represented by a line of print, the lines of print being in the same order as the cards in the deck. Each line of print consists of 80 graphics representing from left to right the information punched in columns 1 through 80 of the corresponding card. To produce this listing we want the computer to read the cards one at a time and print each card on the printer.

For this run we have two files, the card file, which is the INPUT file, and the printer file, which is the OUTPUT file. To tell the RPG that the INPUT file is to be read on the card reader and that the OUTPUT file is to be printed on the printer, the *File Description Form* is used as shown in Figure 4-2. The "I" is entered in column 15 of the File Description Form to indicate to the RPG that the

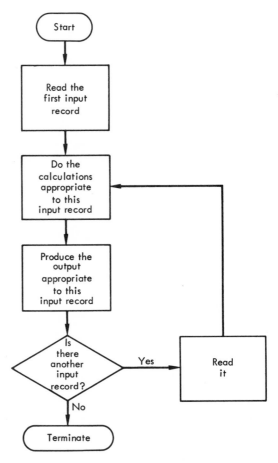

Figure 4-1   RPG object program basic processing cycle.

INPUT file is an input file. The "O" is entered to indicate that the OUTPUT file is an output file.

The input to the run is then described on the *Input Description Form* as shown in Figure 4-3. Input record types are identified in columns 15 through 42 of the Input Description Form, and the fact that there are no entries in these columns indicates that there is only one record type in the INPUT file. The Input Form says that the INPUT file is made up of a series of records, each of which contains one field named CARD that is found in positions 1 through 80 of the record.

RPG FILE DESCRIPTION FORM

Line	Form Type	Filename	File Type	File Designation	End of File	Sequence		Record Length		Key Field Starting Location	Extension Code E/L	Device	
0 1	F	INPUT	I									READ0 I	
0 2	F	OUTPUT	O									PRINTER	
0 3	F												

Figure 4-2 Card listing file description.

RPG INPUT FORM

Line	Form Type	Filename	Sequence	Number (1-N)	Option (O)	Record Identifying Indicator	Record Identification Codes			Field Location		Decimal Positions	Field Name	Control Level (L1-L9)	Matching Fields or Chaining Fields	Field Indicators		
							Position Not (N) C/Z/D Character	Position Not (N) C/Z/D Character	Position Not (N) C/Z/D Character	From	To					Plus	Minus	Zero or Blank
0 1	I	INPUT																
0 2	I									1	80		CARD					
0 3	I																	
0 4	I																	
0 5	I																	

Figure 4-3 Card listing input description.

Finally, the output is described on the *Output Description Form* as shown in Figure 4-4. The Output Description Form says that during each RPG cycle the field CARD is to be printed on the printer. The Input Form specifies that the field CARD is 80 positions long, the Output Form specifies that the last position of the field is to be

RPG OUTPUT DESCRIPTION FORM

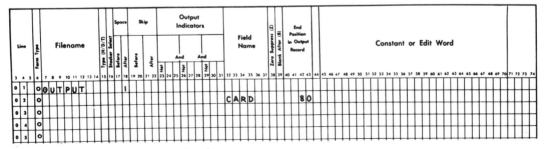

Line	Form Type	Filename	Type (H/D/T)	Stacker Select	Space Before	Space After	Skip Before	Skip After	Output Indicators And Not	And Not	Field Name	Zero Suppress (Z)	Blank After (B)	End Position in Output Record	Constant or Edit Word
0 1	O	OUTPUT			1										
0 2	O										CARD			80	
0 3	O														
0 4	O														
0 5	O														

Figure 4-4 Card listing output description.

```
40246112011426LINEMANS PLIERS, BEVEL NOSE                      6  367
40246112011428SCREWDRIVER, STEEL SHANK                        12   99
40246112011430WRENCH SET, SIX PIECE, OPEN END                12  537
40246112011432PIPE WRENCH, HEAVY DUTY                          3  264
40246113011428SCREWDRIVER, STEEL SHANK                         6   99
40246113011434PLANE, SMOOTH BOTTOM, 9 INCH                     6  780
40246113011436BRACE, HEAVY DUTY, BOX RACHET                    3  720
40246113011438SAW, CROSSCUT, HOLLOW GROUND                     9  986
40246114011430WRENCH SET, SIX PIECE, OPEN END                 3  537
40246114011432PIPE WRENCH, HEAVY DUTY                          6  264
40246114011440HAMMER, CLAW, STEEL HANDLE                      12  485
40246114011442STAPLER, VARIABLE COMPRESSION                   6 1079
40310112011444SLEDGE, DOUBLE FACED                             2  625
40310112011446HATCHET, STEEL HANDLE                            6  587
40310112011448AXE, DOUBLE BIT, HICKORY HANDLE                 6  630
40310112011450SAW, KEYHOLE, 10 INCH BLADE                     6  142
40310113011426LINEMANS PLIERS, BEVEL NOSE                      3  367
40310113011430WRENCH SET, SIX PIECE, OPEN END                 6  537
40369114011434PLANE, SMOOTH BOTTOM, 9 INCH                     3  780
40369114011438SAW, CROSSCUT, HOLLOW GROUND                    12  986
40369114011440HAMMER, CLAW, STEEL HANDLE                      12  485
40369114011444SLEDGE, DOUBLE FACED                             3  625
40369115011448AXE, DOUBLE BIT, HICKORY HANDLE                 2  630
40369115011450SAW, KEYHOLE, 10 INCH BLADE                      3  142
40369115011452SOLDERING IRON, 200 WATT                         3  726
40369115011454WRENCH, ADJUSTABLE END                          12  206
```

Figure 4-5 Card listing.

printed in print position 80 of the printer, and consequently each card is printed in print positions 1 through 80. The Output Form also specifies that after each line of print the paper in the printer is to be advanced one line. As a consequence, the card listing will be single spaced.

On the basis of the above source information the RPG produces an *object program*, which when run produces output as shown in Figure 4-5. As can be seen from the listing, the cards in the deck have information punched in them in columns 1 through 58 only.

5 PRINTER OUTPUT
VERTICAL FORMAT

Printers use *continuous forms*. This means that the paper to be printed on is fed through the printer in one long, continuous strip. The paper is made up of a series of pages, and the pages are marked off by perforations across the continuous strip. The paper is generally folded on these perforations in an accordion fashion, so that the continuous form looks like a pile of single pages. The strip then feeds out into the printer as it is lifted off the pile, as shown in Figure 5-1. The perforation on which the continuous form is folded is the *fan fold*, and after the printing has been done, the paper is separated, or *burst*, along the fanfolds to convert the printed output from one long, continuous form into a series of separate pages.

If a report, such as our card listing, were more than one page long and were printed with single spacing, some of the printing would occur very near or on the fanfold, and this information might very well become illegible when the paper is burst. To avoid this loss of information, it is customary to leave both a blank *heading* and a blank *footing* at the top and bottom, respectively, of each

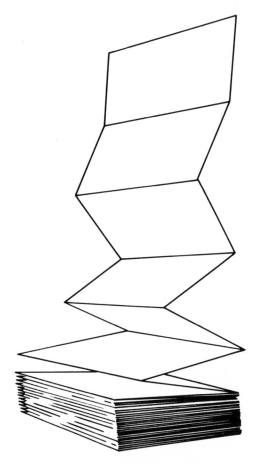

Figure 5-1   Continuous forms.

page. Thus, instead of being printed as shown in Figure 4-5, our card listing might appear as shown in Figure 5-2.

To prepare a report in this form, it is necessary to know when the fanfold is approaching, so a spacing operation to create a footing and a heading can be performed. This is accomplished by means of a *paper loop* in the printer. If the paper loop were cut and straightened out, it would be just as long as a single page. The printer advances the paper loop one line each time the paper is advanced one line. Thus, the loop makes one complete revolution each time a page passes through the printer.

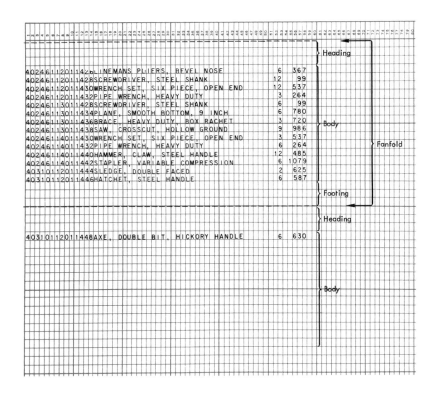

Figure 5-2 Card listing with headings and footings.

The paper loop has a number of columns on it that run the length of the loop parallel to the edge of the loop. Each of these columns is a *channel*. The paper loop also has a number of rows on it, each row corresponding to the middle of a print line on the paper. A paper loop is shown in Figure 5-3.

One of the channels on the paper loop is the *form overflow channel*. If a hole is punched in the paper loop at the intersection of the form overflow channel and the line on which we want the last line on the page to print, then when that line is printed, the RPG object program makes note that it is to set the *form overflow indicator*.*

Once set, the form overflow (OF) indicator remains set for one full processing cycle of the RPG object program, after which it is reset.

---

*Actually, the punch must appear some number of lines before the last line to be printed on the page, but in this book this refinement is ignored.

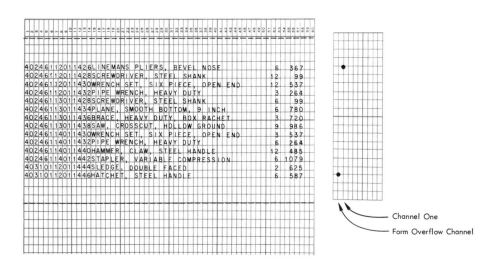

Figure 5-3   The paper loop.

The precise timing of the use of the OF indicator to produce output is shown in Figure 5-4.

The OF indicator can be used to control vertical printing format, as shown in Figure 5-5. Figure 5-5 is the same as Figure 5-4 with the exception of the addition of the third line, which says that when the OF indicator is set, the paper should be spaced an additional five lines. The object program produced from the above output specifications will, when run with the paper loop shown in Figure 5-3, produce the card listing shown in Figure 5-3.

Instead of spacing a large number of lines, the printer can be instructed to feed the paper without printing until a hole is sensed in a specified channel of the paper loop. This is *form feeding* or *skipping paper*. Such a hole is punched in channel 1 of the paper loop shown in Figure 5-3. The coding shown in Figure 5-6 takes advantage of this punch and is equivalent to the coding in Figure 5-5.

In reality the form feeding of paper over the fanfold is such a common operation that, if no provision is made for it in the program, the RPG automatically provides for it. If the OF indicator is not used to condition any printer output, the RPG assumes that no provision for form feeding over the fanfold is being made in the

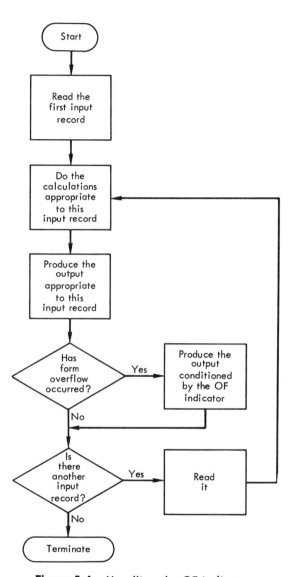

Figure 5-4 Handling the OF indicator.

RPG OUTPUT DESCRIPTION FORM

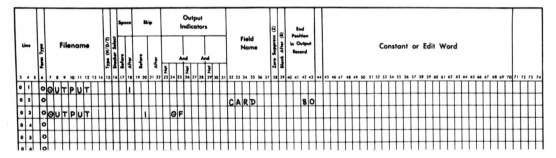

Figure 5-5 Vertical printing format control.

program. The provision that the RPG consequently makes is to form feed to channel 1 on detection of form overflow. Thus, Figure 4-4 is equivalent to Figure 5-6.

RPG OUTPUT DESCRIPTION FORM

Figure 5-6 Form feeding.

6 PRINTER OUTPUT HORIZONTAL FORMAT

Suppose the cards to be listed have the format shown in Figure 6-1. While it is possible to read the cards from the listing

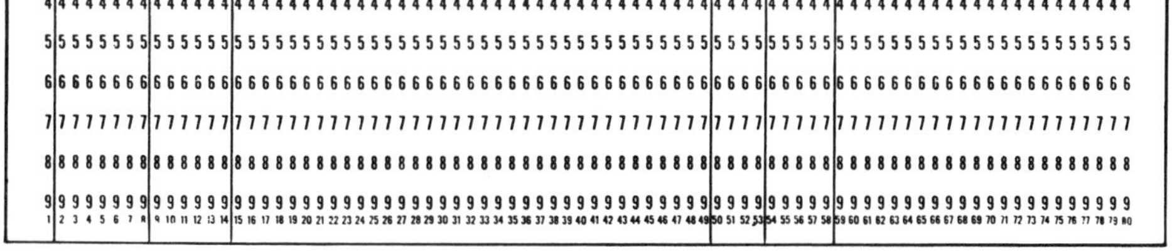

Figure 6-1 Card layout.

Figure 6-2   Card listing by field.

shown in Figure 4-5, the listing shown in Figure 6-2 would be easier to understand. This listing can be produced by describing the fields on the Input and Output Forms as shown in Figures 6-3 and 6-4.

Figure 6-2 is easier to read than Figure 4-5, but the informa-

RPG INPUT FORM

Figure 6-3   Input field description.

RPG OUTPUT DESCRIPTION FORM

Line	Form Type	Filename	Type (H/D/T)	Stacker Select	Space Before	Space After	Skip Before	Skip After	Output Indicators And Not	And Not	Not	Field Name	Zero Suppress (Z)	Blank After (B)	End Position in Output Record	Constant or Edit Word
0 1	O	OUTPUT						1								
0 2	O											TYPE			1	
0 3	O											CUST			9	
0 4	O											ITEM			16	
0 5	O											DESC			53	
0 6	O											QUANT			60	
0 7	O											PRICE			68	
0 8	O															

Figure 6-4 Output field description.

tion would be more meaningful if it were captioned as shown in Figure 6-5. Such output can be obtained from a program generated according to the specifications made on the Output Form shown in Figure 6-6.

Lines 1 and 2 of Figure 6-6 say that, when form overflow occurs, the paper is to be fed to channel 1, the *constant* ITEM is to

```
        ITEM
T  CUST  NUMBER              DESCRIPTION                    QUANTITY  PRICE
4  0246112  011426   LINEMANS PLIERS, BEVEL NOSE                6       367
4  0246112  011428   SCREWDRIVER, STEEL SHANK                  12        99
4  0246112  011430   WRENCH SET, SIX PIECE, OPEN END           12       537
4  0246112  011432   PIPE WRENCH, HEAVY DUTY                     3       264
4  0246113  011428   SCREWDRIVER, STEEL SHANK                    6        99
4  0246113  011434   PLANE, SMOOTH BOTTOM, 9 INCH               6       780
4  0246113  011436   BRACE, HEAVY DUTY, BOX RACHET              3       720
4  0246113  011438   SAW, CROSSCUT, HOLLOW GROUND               9       986
4  0246114  011430   WRENCH SET, SIX PIECE, OPEN END            3       537
4  0246114  011432   PIPE WRENCH, HEAVY DUTY                     6       264
4  0246114  011440   HAMMER, CLAW, STEEL HANDLE                12       485
4  0246114  011442   STAPLER, VARIABLE COMPRESSION              6      1079
4  0310112  011444   SLEDGE, DOUBLE FACED                       2       625
4  0310112  011446   HATCHET, STEEL HANDLE                      6       587
4  0310112  011448   AXE, DOUBLE BIT, HICKORY HANDLE            6       630
4  0310112  011450   SAW, KEYHOLE, 10 INCH BLADE                6       142
4  0310113  011426   LINEMANS PLIERS, BEVEL NOSE                3       367
4  0310113  011430   WRENCH SET, SIX PIECE, OPEN END            6       537
4  0369114  011434   PLANE, SMOOTH BOTTOM, 9 INCH               3       780
4  0369114  011438   SAW, CROSSCUT, HOLLOW GROUND              12       986
4  0369114  011440   HAMMER, CLAW, STEEL HANDLE                12       485
```

Figure 6-5 Card listing with headings.

RPG OUTPUT DESCRIPTION FORM

Line	Form Type	Filename	Type (H,D,T)	Space Before	Space After	Skip Before	Skip After	Output Indicators	Field Name	End Position in Output Record	Constant or Edit Word
01	O	OUTPUT		1		1	1	OF			
02	O									15	'ITEM'
03	O	OUTPUT				2		OF			
04	O									1	'T'
05	O									7	'CUST'
06	O									16	'NUMBER'
07	O									41	'DESCRIPTION'
08	O									62	'QUANTITY'
09	O									68	'PRICE'
10	O	OUTPUT		1							
11	O								TYPE	1	
12	O								CUST	9	
13	O								ITEM	16	
14	O								DESC	53	
15	O								QUANT	60	
16	O								PRICE	68	

Figure 6-6 Output heading description.

be printed in print positions 12 through 15, and the paper is to be spaced one line. Lines 3 through 9 of Figure 6-6 say that, after the above has been done, the constants T, CUST, NUMBER, DESCRIPTION, QUANTITY, and PRICE are to be printed in the specified positions and the paper is then to be spaced two lines. Lines 10 through 16 are familiar to us—they describe the procedure for printing the body of our listing.

Actually, the information in Figure 6-6 is not complete. This Output Form specification will produce the desired output format on all but the first page. On the first page the heading will not be printed, since the OF indicator will not be set. To rectify this situation, a special indicator, the *first page indicator*, is used. The first page (1P) indicator is set when the generated object program is initiated, it remains set long enough to produce headings on the first page of printed output, and it is then reset and remains reset for the remainder of the object program execution. The precise timing of the setting and resetting of the 1P indicator is shown in Figure 6-7. Use of the 1P indicator is shown in Figure 6-8.

Lines 1 through 9 of Figure 6-8 provide for the printing of the heading on the first page. Lines 10 through 18 provide for the printing of the heading when form overflow occurs. Printing of a body line is dependent on the 1P indicator being reset. As a consequence, no body line is printed when the 1P indicator is set, which is the situation when the headings on the first page are being printed and no input card has yet been read.

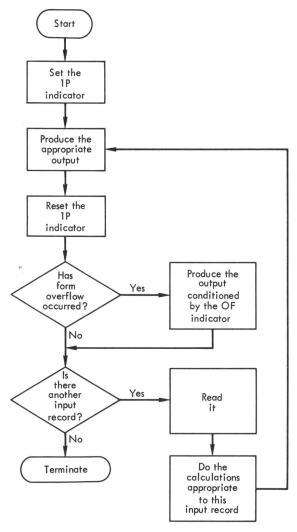

Figure 6-7   Handling the 1P indicator.

RPG OUTPUT DESCRIPTION FORM

Line	Form Type	Filename	Space Before	Skip Before	Output Indicators	Field Name	End Position in Output Record	Constant or Edit Word
01	O	OUTPUT	1	1	1P			
02	O						15	'ITEM'
03	O	OUTPUT	2		1P			
04	O						1	'T'
05	O						7	'CUST'
06	O						16	'NUMBER'
07	O						41	'DESCRIPTION'
08	O						62	'QUANTITY'
09	O						68	'PRICE'
10	O	OUTPUT	1	1	0F			
11	O						15	'ITEM'
12	O	OUTPUT	2		0F			
13	O						1	'T'
14	O						7	'CUST'
15	O						16	'NUMBER'
16	O						41	'DESCRIPTION'
17	O						62	'QUANTITY'
18	O						68	'PRICE'
19	O	OUTPUT	1		N1P			
20	O					TYPE	1	
21	O					CUST	9	
22	O					ITEM	16	
23	O					DESC	53	
24	O					QUANT	60	
25	O					PRICE	68	

Figure 6-8   Using the 1P indicator.

The reset condition of an indicator is specified by preceding the indicator identification with an N. Thus, N1P means "indicator 1P must be reset."

The RPG language provides a shorthand way of stating that an event should occur if one condition or another condition is present. This technique is the OR *condition* and is illustrated in Figure 6-9. The codings in Figures 6-8 and 6-9 are equivalent.

In Figure 6-9 the vertical format specification is the same regardless of which of the OR conditions is satisfied. In such a case, the specification does not have to be repeated. That is, the Output Form in Figure 6-10 is equivalent to the one in Figure 6-9.

Line	Form Type	Filename	Type (H/D/T)	Stacker Select	Space Before	Space After	Skip Before	Skip After	Output Indicators			Field Name	Zero Suppress (Z)	Blank After (B)	End Position in Output Record	Constant or Edit Word
01	O	OUTPUT			1	1					1P					
02	O	OR			1	1					OF					
03	O														15	'ITEM'
04	O	OUTPUT				2					1P					
05	O	OR				2					OF					
06	O														1	'T'
07	O														7	'CUST'
08	O														16	'NUMBER'
09	O														41	'DESCRIPTION'
10	O														62	'QUANTITY'
11	O														68	'PRICE'
12	O	OUTPUT			1						N1P					
13	O											TYPE			1	
14	O											CUST			9	
15	O											ITEM			16	
16	O											DESC			53	
17	O											QUANT			60	
18	O											PRICE			68	

Figure 6-9 The OR condition.

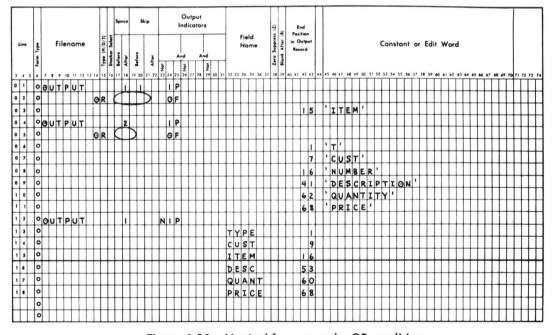

Figure 6-10 Vertical format on the OR condition.

To keep the pages in our card listing straight, it is desirable to number the pages of our listing as shown in Figure 6-11. Page numbering is accomplished by means of a special field named PAGE. PAGE is a field peculiar to the RPG. The RPG object program takes special action with respect to it. Consequently, PAGE is a *restricted name*—it cannot be used to name any other field but a page number. The special action the object program takes with respect to the PAGE field involves, every time it is referenced for output, increasing its contents by one before being put out. Its initial value is zero. Thus, the first time it is put out its value is one, the second time its value is two, the third time three, and so on. Therefore, if it is referenced once per page, it can be used for page numbering. The Output Form used to produce the listing shown in Figure 6-11 is shown in Figure 6-12.

To some it may be undesirable to print zeros in front of a page number. Thus, it is more desirable to print

PAGE 1

than it is to print

PAGE 0001

```
                                                                                                PAGE 0001

           ITEM
T  CUST   NUMBER                DESCRIPTION                          QUANITY PRICE

4 0246112 011426  LINEMANS PLIERS, BEVEL NOSE                              6    367
4 0246112 011428  SCREWDRIVER, STEEL SHANK                                12     99
4 0246112 011430  WRENCH SET, SIX PIECE, OPEN END                         12    537
4 0246112 011432  PIPE WRENCH, HEAVY DUTY                                  3    264
4 0246113 011428  SCREWDRIVER, STEEL SHANK                                 6     99
4 0246113 011434  PLANE, SMOOTH BOTTOM, 9 INCH                             6    780
4 0246113 011436  BRACE, HEAVY DUTY, BOX RACHET                            3    720
4 0246113 011438  SAW, CROSSCUT, HOLLOW GROUND                             9    986
4 0246114 011430  WRENCH SET, SIX PIECE, OPEN END                          3    537
4 0246114 011432  PIPE WRENCH, HEAVY DUTY                                  6    264
4 0246114 011440  HAMMER, CLAW, STEEL HANDLE                              12    485
4 0246114 011442  STAPLER, VARIABLE COMPRESSION                            6   1079
4 0310112 011444  SLEDGE, DOUBLE FACED                                     2    625
4 0310112 011446  HATCHET, STEEL HANDLE                                    6    587
4 0310112 011448  AXE, DOUBLE BIT, HICKORY HANDLE                          6    630
4 0310112 011450  SAW, KEYHOLE, 10 INCH BLADE                              6    142
4 0310113 011426  LINEMANS PLIERS, BEVEL NOSE                              3    367
4 0310113 011430  WRENCH SET, SIX PIECE, OPEN END                          6    537
4 0369114 011434  PLANE, SMOOTH BOTTOM, 9 INCH                             3    780
```

Figure 6-11 Card listing with page numbering.

RPG OUTPUT DESCRIPTION FORM

Line	Form Type	Filename	Type (H.D.T)	Stacker Select	Space Before	Space After	Skip Before	Skip After	Output Indicators Not	And Not	And Not	Field Name	Zero Suppress .Z: Blank After .B)	End Position in Output Record	Constant or Edit Word
0 1	O	OUTPUT			2		1		1 P						
0 2	O	OR							O F						
0 3	O													78	'PAGE'
0 4	O											PAGE		83	
0 5	O	OUTPUT			1				1 P						
0 6	O	OR							O F						
0 7	O													15	'ITEM'
0 8	O	OUTPUT			2				1 P						
0 9	O	OR							O F						
1 0	O													1	'T'
1 1	O													7	'CUST'
1 2	O													16	'NUMBER'
1 3	O													41	'DESCRIPTION'
1 4	O													62	'QUANTITY'
1 5	O													68	'PRICE'
1 6	O	OUTPUT			1				N 1 P						
1 7	O											TYPE		1	
1 8	O											CUST		9	
1 9	O											ITEM		16	
2 0	O											DESC		53	
2 1	O											QUANT		60	
2 2	O											PRICE		68	
	O														
	O														

Figure 6-12   Page numbering.

This can be done by *zero suppressing* the PAGE field as shown in Figure 6-13.

There is a more compelling reason for zero suppressing the PAGE field. The contents of the PAGE field are the result of the arithmetic operation of adding plus one to the PAGE field. Consequently, the PAGE field always carries a plus sign as the zone of its least significant digit. As the PAGE field is incremented, we want it to print out as follows.

$$0001$$
$$0002$$
$$0003$$
$$0004$$
$$0005$$

RPG OUTPUT DESCRIPTION FORM

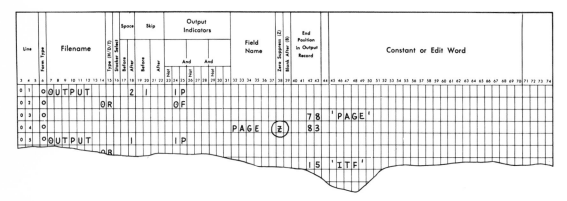

Figure 6-13 Zero suppression.

$$
\begin{array}{c}
0006 \\
0007 \\
0008 \\
0009 \\
0010 \\
0011 \\
0012 \\
\bullet \\
\bullet \\
\bullet
\end{array}
$$

However, if the PAGE field is printed without zero suppression, what is printed is as follows.

$$
\begin{array}{c}
000A \\
000B \\
000C \\
000D \\
000E \\
000F \\
000G \\
000H \\
000I \\
001
\end{array}
$$

001A

001B

.

.

.

We get the alphabetic rather than the numeric in the least significant digit because the least significant digit has a zone of 1100 (plus) rather than 1111. (See Table 2-3.) Zero suppression substitutes the numeric zone for the sign in the least significant digit position. With zero suppression what is printed is as follows.

1
2
3
4
5
6
7
8
9
10
11
12

.

.

.

Value of the PAGE field	PAGE field represented in EBCDIC	Graphic equivalent	PAGE field represented in EBCDIC after zero suppression	Graphic equivalent after zero suppression
1	1111 0000 1111 0000 1111 0000 1100 0001	000A	0100 0000 0100 0000 0100 0000 1111 0001	1
2	1111 0000 1111 0000 1111 0000 1100 0010	000B	0100 0000 0100 0000 0100 0000 1111 0010	2
3	1111 0000 1111 0000 1111 0000 1100 0011	000C	0100 0000 0100 0000 0100 0000 1111 0011	3
4	1111 0000 1111 0000 1111 0000 1100 0100	000D	0100 0000 0100 0000 0100 0000 1111 0100	4
5	1111 0000 1111 0000 1111 0000 1100 0101	000E	0100 0000 0100 0000 0100 0000 1111 0101	5
6	1111 0000 1111 0000 1111 0000 1100 0110	000F	0100 0000 0100 0000 0100 0000 1111 0110	6
7	1111 0000 1111 0000 1111 0000 1100 0111	000G	0100 0000 0100 0000 0100 0000 1111 0111	7
8	1111 0000 1111 0000 1111 0000 1100 1000	000H	0100 0000 0100 0000 0100 0000 1111 1000	8
9	1111 0000 1111 0000 1111 0000 1100 1001	000I	0100 0000 0100 0000 0100 0000 1111 1001	9
10	1111 0000 1111 0000 1111 0001 1100 0000	001	0100 0000 0100 0000 1111 0001 1111 0000	10
11	1111 0000 1111 0000 1111 0001 1100 0001	001A	0100 0000 0100 0000 1111 0001 1111 0001	11
12	1111 0000 1111 0000 1111 0001 1100 0010	001B	0100 0000 0100 0000 1111 0001 1111 0010	12

Figure 6-14 Effect of zero suppression on the page field.

T	CUST	ITEM NUMBER	DESCRIPTION	QUANTITY	PRICE	PAGE
						1
4	0246112	011426	LINEMANS PLIERS, BEVEL NOSE	6	3.67	
4	0246112	011428	SCREWDRIVER, STEEL SHANK	12	.99	
4	0246112	011430	WRENCH SET, SIX PIECE, OPEN END	12	5.37	
4	0246112	011432	PIPE WRENCH, HEAVY DUTY	3	2.64	
4	0246113	011428	SCREWDRIVER, STEEL SHANK	6	.99	
4	0246113	011434	PLANE, SMOOTH BOTTOM, 9 INCH	6	7.80	
4	0246113	011436	BRACE, HEAVY DUTY, BOX RACHET	3	7.20	
4	0246113	011438	SAW, CROSSCUT, HOLLOW GROUND	9	9.86	
4	0246114	011430	WRENCH SET, SIX PIECE, OPEN END	3	5.37	
4	0246114	011432	PIPE WRENCH, HEAVY DUTY	6	2.64	
4	0246114	011440	HAMMER, CLAW, STEEL HANDLE	12	4.85	
4	0246114	011442	STAPLER, VARIABLE COMPRESSION	6	10.79	
4	0310112	011444	SLEDGE, DOUBLE FACED	2	6.25	
4	0310112	011446	HATCHET, STEEL HANDLE	6	5.87	
4	0310112	011448	AXE, DOUBLE BIT, HICKORY HANDLE	6	6.30	
4	0310112	011450	SAW, KEYHOLE, 10 INCH BLADE	6	1.42	
4	0310113	011426	LINEMANS PLIERS, BEVEL NOSE	3	3.67	
4	0310113	011430	WRENCH SET, SIX PIECE, OPEN END	6	5.37	
4	0369114	011434	PLANE, SMOOTH BOTTOM, 9 INCH	3	7.80	

Figure 6-15 Card listing with editing.

Figure 6-14 summarizes the above discussion of the effect of zero suppression on the PAGE field.

Dollar-and-cent figures might be easier to read if they were *edited* as shown in Figure 6-15. The way to accomplish this editing is shown in Figure 6-16. The circled portion of Figure 6-16 contains an *edit word*. It indicates that the first three digits of the field PRICE are to be printed in positions 63, 64, and 65, that a period is to be printed in position 66, and that the last two digits of the field are to be printed in positions 67 and 68. The zero in the edit word indicates that the value to be printed in positions 63, 64, and 65 is to be zero suppressed. Any value that is edited is zero suppressed. The zero indicates the position in the edit word after which zero suppression is to cease if it has not already done so. The zero is the *significance start character*. Possible PRICE values and how they would appear after being edited according to the edit word in Figure 6-16 are shown in Table 6-1.

Table 6-1

Value	Edited value
12345	123.45
02345	23.45
00345	3.45
00045	.45
00005	.05
00000	.00

RPG OUTPUT DESCRIPTION FORM

Line	Form Type	Filename	Type / AND-OR	Space After	Skip Before	Output Indicators	Field Name	Zero Suppress (Z)	End Position in Output Record	Constant or Edit Word
01	O	OUTPUT		2	1	IP				
02	O		OR			OF				
03	O								78	'PAGE'
04	O						PAGE	Z	83	
05	O	OUTPUT		1		IP				
06	O		OR			OF				
07	O								15	'ITEM'
08	O	OUTPUT		2		IP				
09	O		OR			OF				
10	O								1	'T'
11	O								7	'CUST'
12	O								16	'NUMBER'
13	O								41	'DESCRIPTION'
14	O								62	'QUANTITY'
15	O								68	'PRICE'
16	O	OUTPUT		1		NIP				
17	O						TYPE		1	
18	O						CUST		9	
19	O						ITEM		16	
20	O						DESC		53	
21	O						QUANT		60	
22	O						PRICE		68	' 0. '
	O									
	O									
	O									

Figure 6-16 Editing.

EXERCISES

Given a deck of cards with the following layout:

Columns	*Fields*
1	Type
2–6	Employee number
7–36	Name
37–40	Hourly pay rate in tenths of a cent
41, 42, 43	Hours worked in tenths of an hour

List the cards. Place the fields in separate columns. Caption the columns. Number the pages. Edit the pay-rate field.

7 EXTENSION AND SUMMARIZATION

Suppose each word, or *line item*, in our card listing is to have the quantity extended by the price to produce a cost as shown in Figure 7-1. This listing can be produced by using the Input Form

T	CUST	ITEM NUMBER	DESCRIPTION	QUANTITY	PRICE	COST
4	0246112	011426	LINEMANS PLIERS, BEVEL NOSE	6	3.67	22.02
4	0246112	011428	SCREWDRIVER, STEEL SHANK	12	.99	11.88
4	0246112	011430	WRENCH SET, SIX PIECE, OPEN END	12	5.37	64.44
4	0246112	011432	PIPE WRENCH, HEAVY DUTY	3	2.64	7.92
4	0246113	011428	SCREWDRIVER, STEEL SHANK	6	.99	5.94
4	0246113	011434	PLANE, SMOOTH BOTTOM, 9 INCH	6	7.80	46.80
4	0246113	011436	BRACE, HEAVY DUTY, BOX RACHET	3	7.20	21.60
4	0246113	011438	SAW, CROSSCUT, HOLLOW GROUND	9	9.86	88.74
4	0246114	011430	WRENCH SET, SIX PIECE, OPEN END	3	5.37	16.11
4	0246114	011432	PIPE WRENCH, HEAVY DUTY	6	2.64	15.84
4	0246114	011440	HAMMER, CLAW, STEEL HANDLE	12	4.85	58.20
4	0246114	011442	STAPLER, VARIABLE COMPRESSION	6	10.79	64.74
4	0310112	011444	SLEDGE, DOUBLE FACED	2	6.25	12.50
4	0310112	011446	HATCHET, STEEL HANDLE	6	5.87	35.22
4	0310112	011448	AXE, DOUBLE BIT, HICKORY HANDLE	6	6.30	37.80
4	0310112	011450	SAW, KEYHOLE, 10 INCH BLADE	6	1.42	8.52
4	0310113	011426	LINEMANS PLIERS, BEVEL NOSE	3	3.67	11.01
4	0310113	011430	WRENCH SET, SIX PIECE, OPEN END	6	5.37	32.22
4	0369114	011434	PLANE, SMOOTH BOTTOM, 9 INCH	3	7.80	23.40

PAGE 1

Figure 7-1 Card listing with extension.

84

shown in Figure 7-2, the *Calculation Form* shown in Figure 7-3, and the Output Form shown in Figure 7-4.

RPG INPUT FORM

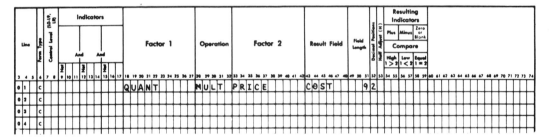

Figure 7-2 Numeric field description.

RPG CALCULATION FORM

Figure 7-3 Calculation.

The new form is the Calculation Form. It is used to specify that, for each card, the QUANT field is to be multiplied by the PRICE field to produce a new field named COST. The Calculation Form says that the COST field is nine digits long and has a decimal point positioned in it two digits from the right. The decimal point does not actually appear in the COST field any more than it appears in the PRICE field. The decimal point information merely tells the object program how to position the result of the multiplication in the COST field. To do this positioning the program must know where the decimal points are in the QUANT and PRICE fields. This information

RPG OUTPUT DESCRIPTION FORM

Line	Form Type	Filename	Type (H/D/T)	Stacker Select	Space Before	Space After	Skip Before	Skip After	Output Indicators (And / And)	Field Name	Zero Suppress (Z) / Blank After (B)	End Position in Output Record	Constant or Edit Word
01	O	OUTPUT			2	1			1 P				
02	O	OR							0 F				
03	O											78	'PAGE'
04	O									PAGE	Z	83	
05	O	OUTPUT			1				1 P				
06	O	OR							0 F				
07	O											15	'ITEM'
08	O	OUTPUT			2				1 P				
09	O	OR							0 F				
10	O											1	'T'
11	O											7	'CUST'
12	O											16	'NUMBER'
13	O											41	'DESCRIPTION'
14	O											62	'QUANTITY'
15	O											68	'PRICE'
16	O											79	'COST'
17	O	OUTPUT			1				N1P				
18	O									TYPE		1	
19	O									CUST		9	
20	O									ITEM		16	
21	O									DESC		53	
22	O									QUANT	Z	60	
23	O									PRICE		68	' 0. '
24	O									COST		83	' , , 0. '

Figure 7-4 Extension.

is supplied on the Input Form as shown in the circled portion of Figure 7-2.*

---

*In most computers it is necessary to distinguish between *alphabetic* and *numeric* fields. A numeric field contains nothing but numerics; an alphabetic field may contain any character. The RPG does this for input fields on the basis of whether a decimal point position is specified for a field. If a position is specified, the field is numeric; if not, it is alphabetic. Thus, TYPE, CUST, ITEM, and DESC are alphabetic fields, and QUANT and PRICE are numeric. Only numeric fields can be edited. Consequently, to be technically correct, the Output Form in Figure 6-15 would have to be used with the Input Form in Figure 7-2 rather than the one in Figure 6-3.

Most of the information in Figure 7-4 is familiar to us. New information is as follows.

1. Line 16 is used to produce the caption COST.
2. On line 22, QUANT is zero suppressed before being printed. This is because QUANT now enters a calculation operation (see Figure 7-3), and consequently it is given a sign in preparation for this operation. If it were not then subsequently zero suppressed, the sign would cause an alphabetic rather than the appropriate least significant digit of QUANT to be printed, in a manner similar to the situation that is summarized with respect to the PAGE field in Figure 6-14.
3. Line 24 is used to produce the COST figure for each line item in the listing.

The COST figure is edited. Possible COST values and how they would appear after being edited are as shown in Table 7-1. Table 7-1 demonstrates two more characteristics of editing.

Table 7-1

Value	Edited values
12345678I	1,234,567.89
02345678I	234,567.89
00345678I	34,567.89
00045678I	4,567.89
00005678I	567.89
00000678I	67.89
00000078I	7.89
00000008I	.89
00000000I	.09

1. As long as zero suppression is going on, not only are the zeros in the value suppressed, but any special characters, such as comma, in the edit word are also suppressed.
2. Like any other computed value, the COST value carries a

sign, indicated by the character I appearing instead of the digit 9. Just as in zero suppression, the editing of a value substitutes the numeric zone for the sign.

Instead of a straight card listing, it might be desirable to summarize cost by customer as shown in Figure 7-5. To do this it is necessary to understand the concept of a *level break*. A level break occurs when the value of the *control field* on which a listing is being made changes. In our card listing, the customer identification number is the control field. When the RPG object program reads a card on which the value of the CUST field is different from its value on the previous card, a level break occurs. The specification of a control field is shown in Figure 7-6.

The specification of a control field also involves the specification of an indicator that is set when a level break occurs. Such an indicator is a *level break indicator*, and it can be used to control calculations and output the same way the OF and 1P indicators can. In the case of Figure 7-6, the level break indicator specified is indicator L1.

All the calculations and output described so far in this book are done at *detail time*. When a level break occurs, it allows calcu-

T	CUST	ITEM NUMBER	DESCRIPTION	QUANTITY	PRICE	COST
						PAGE 1
4	0246112	011426	LINEMANS PLIERS, BEVEL NOSE	6	3.67	22.02
4	0246112	011428	SCREWDRIVER, STEEL SHANK	12	.99	11.88
4	0246112	011430	WRENCH SET, SIX PIECE, OPEN END	12	5.37	64.44
4	0246112	011432	PIPE WRENCH, HEAVY DUTY	3	2.64	7.92
				AMOUNT		$106.26
4	0246113	011428	SCREWDRIVER, STEEL SHANK	6	.99	5.94
4	0246113	011434	PLANE, SMOOTH BOTTOM, 9 INCH	6	7.80	46.80
4	0246113	011436	BRACE, HEAVY DUTY, BOX RACHET	3	7.20	21.60
4	0246113	011438	SAW, CROSSCUT, HOLLOW GROUND	9	9.86	88.74
				AMOUNT		$163.08
4	0246114	011430	WRENCH SET, SIX PIECE, OPEN END	3	5.37	16.11
4	0246114	011432	PIPE WRENCH, HEAVY DUTY	6	2.64	15.84
4	0246114	011440	HAMMER, CLAW, STEEL HANDLE	12	4.85	58.20
4	0246114	011442	STAPLER, VARIABLE COMPRESSION	6	10.79	64.74
				AMOUNT		$154.89

Figure 7-5 Card listing with summarization.

RPG INPUT FORM

Line	Form Type	Filename	Sequence	Number (1-N)	Option (O)	Resulting Indicator	Record Identification Codes																Field Location		Decimal Positions	Field Name	Control Level (L1-L9)	Matching Fields or Chaining Fields	Field Indicators		
							1				2				3								From	To					Plus	Minus	Zero or Blank
							Position	Not (N)	C/Z/D	Character	Position	Not (N)	C/Z/D	Character	Position	Not (N)	C/Z/D	Character													
0 1	I	I N P U T																								T Y P E					
0 2	I																						1		1	T Y P E					
0 3	I																						2	8		C U S T	L1				
0 4	I																						9	1 4		I T E M					
0 5	I																						1 5	4 9		D E S C					
0 6	I																						5 0	5 3	0	Q U A N T					
0 7	I																						5 4	5 8	2	P R I C E					
0 8	I																														
0 9	I																														
1 0	I																														

Figure 7-6   Control field specification.

lations and output to be done at *total time*. The relation of detail time and total time is shown in Figure 7-7. Three things of note in Figure 7-7 are as follows.

1. Although the reading of a record may cause a level break to occur, the record is not made available for processing until after the total time processing caused by the level break. As a consequence, each record is always processed within its own *control group*.
2. The occurrence of a level break is recognized when the first card containing a control field is read. As a consequence, the level break indicators are set for the first card of the first control group just as they are for the first card of all other control groups. However, the first time level break indicators are set, total time is bypassed to avoid the improper production of totals.
3. When processing indicates that there are no more input records to process, processing does not immediately stop. Instead, the level break indicators are set, and total time is performed. This guarantees the production of the appropriate totals for the last control group.

Figures 7-8 and 7-9 show the Calculation and Output Forms

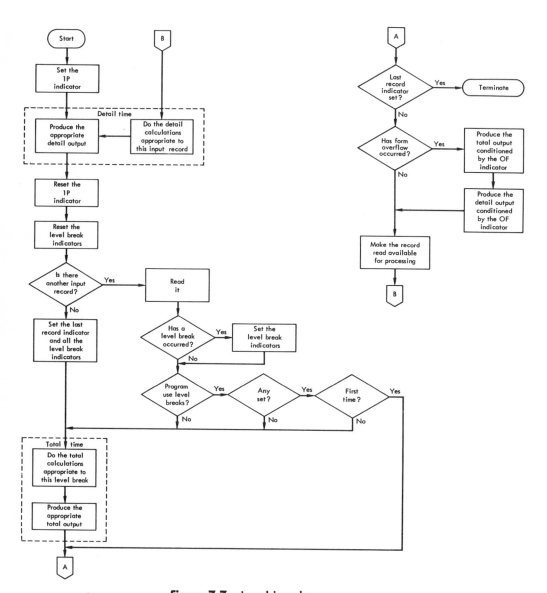

Figure 7-7   Level breaks.

RPG CALCULATION FORM

Line	Form Type	Control Level	Indicators (And / And)	Factor 1	Operation	Factor 2	Result Field	Field Length	Decimal Positions	Half Adjust (H)	Resulting Indicators
0 1	C			QUANT	MULT	PRICE	COST	9 2			
0 2	C			AMT	ADD	COST	AMT	12 2			
0 3	C										
0 4	C										
0 5	C										
0 6	C										
0 7	C										
0 8	C										
0 9	C										
1 0	C										

Figure 7-8 Summarization.

RPG OUTPUT DESCRIPTION FORM

Line	Form Type	Filename	Type (H/D/T)	Stacker Select	Space Before	Space After	Skip Before	Skip After	Output Indicators (And / And)	Field Name	Zero Suppress (Z) Blank After (B)	End Position in Output Record	Constant or Edit Word
0 1	O	OUTPUT			2	1			1P				
0 2	O		OR						OF				
0 3	O											78	'PAGE'
0 4	O									PAGE	Z	83	
0 5	O	OUTPUT			1				1P				
0 6	O		OR						OF				
0 7	O											15	'ITEM'
0 8	O	OUTPUT			2				1P				
0 9	O		OR						OF				
1 0	O											1	'T'
1 1	O											7	'CUST'
1 2	O											16	'NUMBER'
1 3	O											41	'DESCRIPTION'
1 4	O											62	'QUANTITY'
1 5	O											68	'PRICE'
1 6	O											79	'COST'
1 7	O	OUTPUT			1				N1P				
1 8	O									TYPE		1	
1 9	O									CUST		9	
2 0	O									ITEM		16	
2 1	O									DESC		53	
2 2	O									QUANT	Z	60	
2 3	O									PRICE		68	' 0.'
2 4	O									COST		83	' , , 0. '
2 5	O	OUTPUT	T	1	2				L1				
2 6	O											66	'AMOUNT'
2 7	O									AMT	B	83	' , , $0. '

Figure 7-9 Printing totals.

required to produce the totals shown in Figure 7-5. The second line on the Calculation Form says that each time a cost is calculated, it is to be accumulated in a field named AMT. The last three lines on the Output Form say that during total time (signified by the T in column 15), a constant AMOUNT and the AMT field are to be printed if indicator L1 is set. In the AMT field's edit word, the dollar sign just to the left of the significance start character indicates that, in the output, a dollar sign is to be printed just to the left of the first character to be printed in the field. Such an operation is a *floating dollar sign*. Table 7-2 shows some sample amounts and how the dollar sign would be floated for them.

To accumulate amounts correctly, the AMT field must be set to zero at the beginning of the accumulation for a control group. For the first group, the value of zero is assured by the RPG object program—all numeric fields, such as COST and AMT, are set to zero when the program is initiated. For all subsequent groups, the value of zero is provided by the entry B in column 39 of the Output Form. This is a *blank after entry*. It says that after a field (such as AMT) is put out, it is to be blanked, or reset to zero. Thus, after an accumulation is printed, it is set back to zero in preparation for the next accumulation.

The listing in Figure 7-10 eliminates redundant customer information. Such a listing is a *group-indicated* listing. Figure 7-11

Table 7-2

Value	Edited value
01234567891B	$123,456,789.12
00234567891B	$23,456,789.12
00034567891B	$3,456,789.12
00004567891B	$456,789.12
00000567891B	$56,789.12
00000067891B	$6,789.12
00000007891B	$789.12
00000000891B	$89.12
00000000091B	$9.12
00000000001B	$.12
00000000000B	$.02

T	CUST	ITEM NUMBER	DESCRIPTION	QUANTITY	PRICE	COST
4	0246112	011426	LINEMANS PLIERS, BEVEL NOSE	6	3.67	22.02
		011428	SCREWDRIVER, STEEL SHANK	12	.99	11.88
		011430	WRENCH SET, SIX PIECE, OPEN END	12	5.37	64.44
		011432	PIPE WRENCH, HEAVY DUTY	3	2.64	7.92
			AMOUNT			$106.26
4	0246113	011428	SCREWDRIVER, STEEL SHANK	6	.99	5.94
		011434	PLANE, SMOOTH BOTTOM, 9 INCH	6	7.80	46.80
		011436	BRACE, HEAVY DUTY, BOX RACHET	3	7.20	21.60
		011438	SAW, CROSSCUT, HOLLOW GROUND	9	9.86	88.74
			AMOUNT			$163.08
4	0246114	011430	WRENCH SET, SIX PIECE, OPEN END	3	5.37	16.11
		011432	PIPE WRENCH, HEAVY DUTY	6	2.64	15.84
		011440	HAMMER, CLAW, STEEL HANDLE	12	4.85	58.20
		011442	STAPLER, VARIABLE COMPRESSION	6	10.79	64.79
			AMOUNT			$154.89

PAGE 1

Figure 7-10 Group-indicated card listing.

shows how it is produced. Line 17 of Figure 7-11 guarantees that a line item is printed for each card read. However, the circled *condition indicators* in Figure 7-11 allow the TYPE and CUST fields to be printed only for the first line item of each control group.

In some instances it is advantageous to print the information pertaining to each customer on a separate page, as shown in Figure 7-12. To create this listing a new paper loop is needed. The required loop is also shown in Figure 7-12.

The Output Form required to produce this listing is shown in Figure 7-13. The circled section of line 25 of Figure 7-13 guarantees that anytime an amount accumulation is to be printed, the paper is first form fed to channel 2, which causes all totals to be printed at the bottom of the page. Notice that, instead of the first page indicator, the L1 indicator is used to print the heading on the first page. The OF indicator is used to print a heading on the second and subsequent pages of the listing for any one customer—this would be the case if there were more cards for one customer than can be listed on one page. The circled sections of lines 2, 6, and 9 of Figure 7-13 assure that after the amount accumulation has been printed for one customer, the captions will be printed at the top of the next page for the next customer. Notice that after the accumulation for a customer is printed, the paper is not positioned, since the next thing to be printed is a header and the paper will be positioned before printing the header. Also notice that the OF indicator is used to print headings only if the L1 indicator is not set. (See circled portions of lines 1, 5, and 8.) This arrangement is to avoid the possible printing of the heading on one page twice, which would otherwise happen if the OF and L1 indicators were set at the same time.

Lines 1, 5, and 8 are examples of the AND *condition* use of

RPG OUTPUT DESCRIPTION FORM

Line	Form Type	Filename	Type (H/D/T)	Stacker Select	Space Before	Space After	Skip Before	Skip After	Output Indicators And/And/Not	Field Name	Zero Suppress (Z)	Blank After (B)	End Position in Output Record	Constant or Edit Word
01	O	OUTPUT			2	1			I P					
02	O	OR							OF					
03	O												78	'PAGE'
04	O									PAGE	Z		83	
05	O	OUTPUT			1				I P					
06	O	OR							OF					
07	O												15	'ITEM'
08	O	OUTPUT			2				I P					
09	O	OR							OF					
10	O												1	'T'
11	O												7	'CUST'
12	O												16	'NUMBER'
13	O												41	'DESCRIPTION'
14	O												62	'QUANTITY'
15	O												68	'PRICE'
16	O												79	'COST'
17	O	OUTPUT			1				N I P					
18	O								L1	TYPE			1	
19	O								L1	CUST			9	
20	O									ITEM			16	
21	O									DESC			53	
22	O									QUANT	Z		60	
23	O									PRICE			68	' 0. '
24	O									COST			83	' , , 0. '
25	O	OUTPUT	T		1	2			L1					
26	O												66	'AMOUNT'
27	O									AMT		B	83	' , , , $0. '

Figure 7-11   Group-indicated output.

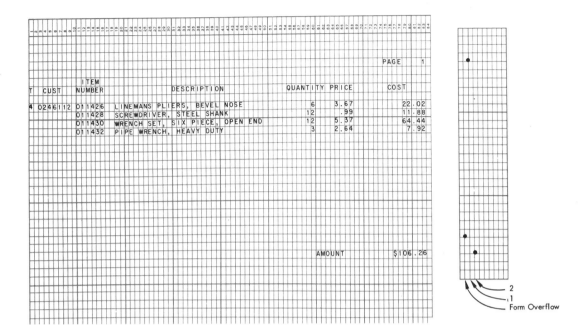

Figure 7-12   Customer per page listing.

indicators for conditioning output. The output described is produced only if all of the indicator conditions specified are satisfied.

Our listing is now organized by customer. Consequently, instead of numbering pages in the listing from beginning to end, it might be desirable to start the numbering of the pages for each customer from 1. The RPG provides the ability to set the page number back to 1 via the condition indicators. If on the Output Form the PAGE field is conditioned by indicators, the PAGE field is set back to 1 rather than incremented by 1 before being printed whenever the conditions are satisfied (that is, whenever the specified indicators are set). Figure 7-14 shows how this feature of the RPG can be used to start the numbering of pages from 1 for each customer. The circled portion of Figure 7-14 assures that whenever a heading is printed because of a change in customer identification number, the page number is set back to 1 before being printed in the heading.

Line	Form Type	Filename	Type (H/D/T)	Stacker Select	Space Before	Space After	Skip Before	Skip After	Output Indicators	Field Name	Zero Suppress (Z) / Blank After (B)	End Position in Output Record	Constant or Edit Word
01	O	OUTPUT			2	1			OF NL1				
02	O	OR							L1				
03	O											78	'PAGE'
04	O									PAGE	Z	83	
05	O	OUTPUT				1			OF NL1				
06	O	OR							L1				
07	O											15	'ITEM'
08	O	OUTPUT				2			OF NL1				
09	O	OR							L1				
10	O											1	'T'
11	O											7	'CUST'
12	O											16	'NUMBER'
13	O											41	'DESCRIPTION'
14	O											62	'QUANTITY'
15	O											68	'PRICE'
16	O											79	'COST'
17	O	OUTPUT				1			N1P				
18	O								L1	TYPE		1	
19	O								L1	CUST		9	
20	O									ITEM		16	
21	O									DESC		53	
22	O									QUANT	Z	60	
23	O									PRICE		68	' 0. '
24	O									COST		83	' , , 0. '
25	O	OUTPUT	T				(2)		L1				
26	O											66	'AMOUNT'
27	O									AMT	B	83	' , , $0. '

Figure 7-13 Customer per page output.

Line	Form Type	Filename	Type (H/D/T)	Stacker Select	Space Before	Space After	Skip Before	Skip After	Output Indicators	Field Name	Zero Suppress (Z) / Blank After (B)	End Position in Output Record	Constant or Edit Word
01	O	OUTPUT			2	1			OF NL1				
02	O	OR							L1				
03	O											78	'PAGE'
04	O								L1	PAGE	Z	83	
05	O	OUTPUT				1			OF NL1				

Figure 7-14 Presetting the page number.

SUMMARY AND ORIENTATION

Chapter 1 presented an overview of data processing that concluded with a description of how the computer is used in data processing. Chapter 2 discussed the ways information is represented for processing by computers. Chapter 3 introduced the concept of a programming language processor. Chapters 4 through 7 presented details of a specific programming language, the RPG language.

The final four chapters detail the way RPG language is used to

1. Describe the fields of a record of an input file in terms of their position in the record, length, alphabetic or numeric character, and decimal point position.
2. Identify, in the input record, fields for level break purposes.
3. Describe the calculations required to do extensions and summarization.
4. Control the format of printed output with respect to
    (a) When to start a new page.
    (b) Provision of headings.
    (c) Positioning of information on the page both vertically and horizontally.
    (d) Editing of information.
    (e) Page numbering.

With these tools a program can be written to read almost any type of file of data records and prepare a report on the information to be found in the file. A significant part of computer data processing consists of this type of operation, as is indicated by the repeated reference in the latter part of Chapter 1 to the need for a printer to produce management reports from the processing of the master file in the simplified inventory application.

In Chapters 4 through 7 the file of data being used as input to the report preparation was a card file. However, it could as easily be a tape or disk file. All files—card, tape, and disk—are formatted into a series of records, the record format is described on the Input Form, and the only change required is the identification of the device handling the file as a card READer, TAPE, or DISK unit on the File Description Form.

EXERCISE

Given a deck of cards with the following layout:

Columns	Fields
1	Type
2–6	Employee number
7–36	Name
37–40	Hourly pay rate in tenths of a cent
41, 42, 43	Hours worked in tenths of an hour

The cards are in order by employee number. The first two digits of the employee number are a department number.

For each card, extend the hours worked by the pay rate to yield gross pay.

Produce a line item for each card. On this line, print employee number, name, pay rate, hours worked, and gross pay in appropriately labeled columns. Summarize gross pay by department. Print the information pertaining to each department on a separate page.

8 MULTIPLE CARD TYPES

So far all cards in the input deck with which we have been dealing have been of the same type. Specifically, they have all had a 4 punch in column 1. It is possible to have more than one card type in a deck. For example, in addition to the card deck having detail cards identified by a 4 punch in column 1, the deck might also have name-and-address cards identified by a 2 punch, and ship-to cards identified by a 1 punch. Both new card types have the same layout, which is shown in Figure 8-1.

The cards are arranged in the deck in the following way. First there is a ship-to card for a customer. Then there is a name-and-address card for the same customer. Finally, there are detail cards for this customer. Following the cards in this customer group are the ship-to, name-and-address, and detail cards for the next customer, and so on. If the address to which the items described on the detail cards are to be shipped is the same as the one on the name-and-address card, the ship-to card for the customer does not appear in the deck. The ship-to card is an *optional card*; the other cards are *required*.

This input deck is described on the Input Form in Figure 8-2.

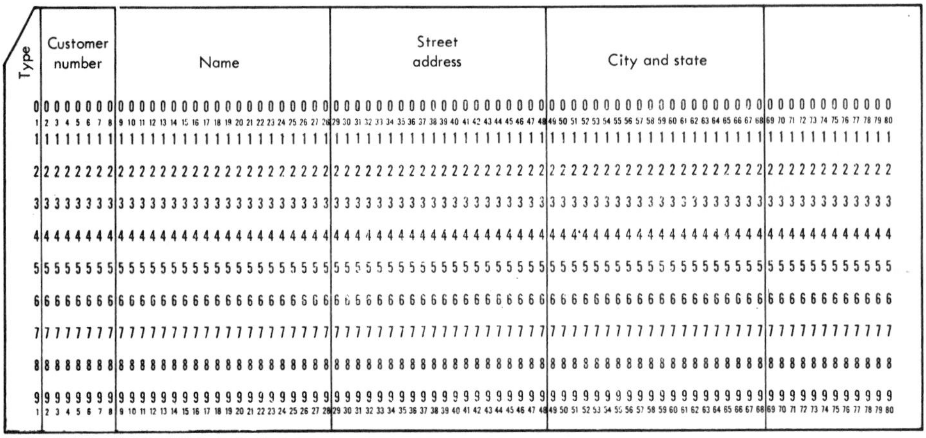

Figure 8-1 Name-and-address and ship-to card layout.

RPG INPUT FORM

Figure 8-2 Multiple input types.

Line 1 of Figure 8-2 says that the first card in a customer group is a ship-to card (01 in columns 15 and 16), that there can be a maximum of one ship-to card in a control group (1 in column 17), that the presence of a ship-to card in a customer group is optional (O in column 18), and that a ship-to card can be recognized by a 1 punch (1 in column 27) in column 1 (1 in columns 21 through 24). The C in column 26 indicates that the 1 appears in the whole column as opposed to appearing in just the digit portion of the column with the zone portion of the column containing some other information.

The 01 in columns 19 and 20 indicates that when a ship-to card is read, an indicator numbered 1 is to be set. Such an indicator is a *record indicator* and can be used to condition calculations and output in the same manner as the OF, 1P, and level indicators are used. There are 99 indicators, numbered 01 through 99, that can be used as record indicators. Lines 2 through 5 describe the fields on a ship-to card.

Line 6 says that the next card in a customer group is a name-and-address card, that there can be only one name-and-address card in a customer group, that a name-and-address card can be recognized by a 2 punch in column 1, and that when a name-and-address card is to be processed, record indicator 2 is to be set. The name-and-address card is a required card since it is not identified as an optional one. Lines 7 through 10 describe the fields on a name-and-address card.

Notice that since the ship-to card is optional, the customer identification number of either a ship-to or a name-and-address card may cause a level break. This is indicated by the L1 level break entry for the customer number field of both the ship-to and the name-and-address cards.

Line 11 says that following the name-and-address card in a customer group are one or more detail cards (N in column 17), that detail cards are identified by a 4 punch in column 1, and that when a detail card is to be processed record indicator 4 is to be set. Lines 12 through 16 are familiar to us and describe the fields on a detail card.

Notice that the customer number field of the detail card is still coded to cause a level break. Such an event should not occur, since all detail cards in a customer group should have the same customer identification number. This coding is an example of a data validation operation built into a processing program. If by mistake detail cards with more than one customer number were to follow a combination of ship-to and name-and-address cards, both record indicator 4 and level break indicator L1 will be set at the same time. How this fact is used to indicate an error is shown in Figure 8-4.

From this input a set of invoices can be produced. The invoices are shown in Figure 8-3 and are not greatly different from the card listing shown in Figure 7-12. The Calculation and Output Forms required to produce the invoices are shown in Figures 8-4 and 8-5.

There are two new things on the Calculation Form. One is that the calculations on lines 1 and 2 are conditioned by record indicator 4. In this way the calculations are done only when a detail record is being processed. They are not done when a ship-to or name-and-address record is being processed.

The other new thing on the Calculation Form is the third line of code. This line says that in the error situation in which both record indicator 4 and level indicator L1 are set, an indicator called a *halt indicator* and named H1 is to be set.

This use of the H1 indicator is an example of a *resulting indicator*. A resulting indicator is set as the result of a calculation oper-

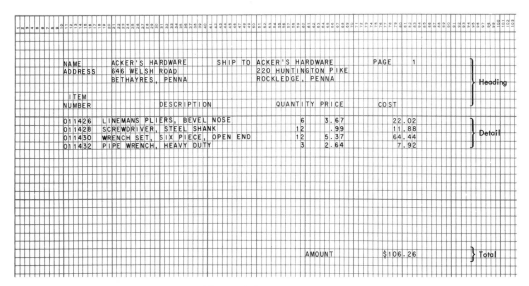

Figure 8-3   Invoice.

RPG CALCULATION FORM

Line	Form Type	Control Level	Indicators And Not	And Not	Factor 1	Operation	Factor 2	Result Field	Field Length	Decimal Positions	Half Adjust (H)	Resulting Indicators Plus/High 1>2	Minus/Low 1<2	Zero or Blank/Equal 1=2
01	C	04			QUANT	MULT	PRICE	COST	92					
02	C	04			AMT	ADD	COST	AMT	122					
03	C	04	L1			SETON						H1		
04	C													
05	C													
06	C													
07	C													
08	C													

Figure 8-4 Invoice calculations.

RPG OUTPUT DESCRIPTION FORM

Line	Form Type	Filename	Type (H/D/T)	Stacker Select	Space Before	Space After	Skip Before	Skip After	Output Indicators And	And Not	Field Name	Zero Suppress (Z) Blank After (B)	End Position in Output Record	Constant or Edit Word
01	O	OUTPUT			1	1			02					
02	O		OR						0FN02					
03	O												14	'NAME'
04	O										NAME		40	
05	O												49	'SHIP TO'
06	O										NAMEA	B	70	
07	O												78	'PAGE'
08	O								02		PAGE	Z	83	
09	O	OUTPUT			1				02					
10	O		OR						0FN02					
11	O												17	'ADDRESS'
12	O										ADDR		40	
13	O										ADDRA	B	70	
14	O	OUTPUT			2				02					
15	O		OR						0FN02					
16	O										CITY		40	
17	O										CITYA	B	70	
18	O	OUTPUT			1				02					
19	O		OR						0FN02					
20	O												15	'ITEM'
21	O	OUTPUT			2				02					
22	O		OR						0FN02					
23	O												16	'NUMBER'
24	O												41	'DESCRIPTION'
25	O												62	'QUANTITY'

Figure 8-5, page 1 Invoice output.

ation, and like the OF, 1P, level, and record indicators it can be used to condition subsequent calculation and output operations. In addition to halt indicators, the indicators numbered 01 through 99 (which are used as record indicators) may be used as resulting indicators. Once a resulting indicator is set, it remains set until a subsequent calculation resets it.

A halt indicator is different from the numbered indicators in that once it is set it is never automatically reset. Moreover, when a halt indicator is set, the RPG object program comes to a halt at the end of the production of detail output in the processing cycle during which the halt indicator was set. Thus, a halt indicator is generally set to indicate the presence of an error, such as the presence of more than one customer number in a group of detail records. There are two halt indicators, named H1 and H2.

Line 3 of Figure 8-4 says that if a detail record is being processed (04 in columns 10 and 11) *and* the customer number has changed (L1 in columns 13 and 14), the H1 halt indicator is to be set. Thus, if a group of detail records contains more than one customer number, the H1 indicator is set. Line 3 of Figure 8-4 is an example of the AND condition use of indicators for conditioning calculations.

RPG OUTPUT DESCRIPTION FORM

Line	Form Type	Filename	Type (H/D/T)	Stacker Select	Space Before	Space After	Skip Before	Skip After	Output Indicators		And		And		Field Name	Zero Suppress (Z)	Blank After (B)	End Position in Output Record	Constant or Edit Word
0 1	O																	6 8	'PRICE'
0 2	O																	7 9	'COST'
0 3	O	OUTPUT							I			04		NH1					
0 4	O														ITEM			1 6	
0 5	O														DESC			5 3	
0 6	O														QUANT	Z		6 0	
0 7	O														PRICE			6 8	' 0. '
0 8	O														COST			8 3	' , , 0. '
0 9	O	OUTPUT	T			2			L1					NH1					
1 0	O																	6 6	'AMOUNT'
1 1	O														AMT	B		8 3	' , , $0. '
1 2	O																		
1 3	O																		
1 4	O																		

Figure 8-5, page 2 Invoice output.

RPG OUTPUT DESCRIPTION FORM

Figure 8-6 Preprinted form output.

All of page 1 and lines 1 and 2 of page 2 of Figure 8-5 are concerned with producing the heading of the invoice. A heading is produced when record indicator 2 is set (first page of an invoice for a customer whose name and address record is now being processed) or when the OF indicator is set (second or following page of an invoice for a customer).

Notice that the ship-to fields (NAMEA, ADDRA, and CITYA) are blanked after printing (B in column 39). Since these are alphabetic fields rather than numeric fields, the operation of blanking after sets the fields to spaces rather than zeros. Because the ship-to fields are blanked after printing, they are printed on only the first page of an invoice. Moreover, if a customer group contains no ship-to card, the ship-to fields are also blank when they are printed on the first page of the customer's invoice. This is the situation even if the first

customer group contains no ship-to card, since all alphabetic fields
are set to spaces when the RPG object program is initiated.

Resetting the page number to 1 for each customer group is
done by use of record indicator 2, which indicates the beginning of
a customer group for output purposes. Lines 3 through 8 of page 2
of Figure 8-5 control printing of the detail lines, and lines 9 through
11 control printing of the total line. The H1 indicator is used to
prevent the production of output in an error situation.

In many instances, constant information is preprinted on the
paper stock used for producing output. In such an instance, the
Output Form shown in Figure 8-6 would be adequate for producing
invoices. Line 10 of Figure 8-6 calls for paper spacing of five lines.
Generally, it is faster to form feed than it is to space more than two
lines. Figure 8-7 shows a preprinted form and a paper loop to be
used with it. The Output Form shown in Figure 8-8 takes advantage
of this paper loop, as indicated in the circled portion.

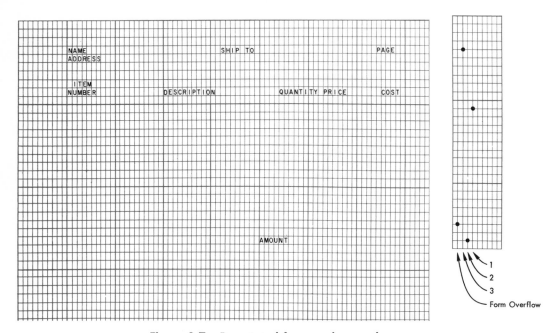

Figure 8-7   Preprinted form and paper loop.

RPG OUTPUT DESCRIPTION FORM

Line	Form Type	Filename	Type (H/D/T)	Stacker Select	Space Before	Space After	Skip Before	Skip After	Output Indicators	Field Name	Zero Suppress (Z)	Blank After (B)	End Position in Output Record	Constant or Edit Word
01	O	OUTPUT				1		1	02					
02	O			OR					OFNO2					
03	O									NAME			40	
04	O									NAMEA		B	70	
05	O								02	PAGE	Z		83	
06	O	OUTPUT				1			02					
07	O			OR					OFNO2					
08	O									ADDR			40	
09	O									ADDRA		B	70	
10	O	OUTPUT					(3)		02					
11	O			OR					OFNO2					
12	O									CITY			40	
13	O									CITYA		B	70	
14	O	OUTPUT				1			04NH1					
15	O									ITEM			16	
16	O									DESC			53	
17	O									QUANT	Z		60	
18	O									PRICE			68	' 0. '
19	O									COST			83	' , , 0. '
20	O	OUTPUT	T			2			LINH1					
21	O									AMT		B	83	' , , , $0. '

Figure 8-8 Form feed to detail printing.

SUMMARY AND ORIENTATION

The new idea introduced in this chapter is the concept of multiple record types in one input file. Such a file is typically organized into a series of *header* records followed by one or more *trailer* or *detail* records. In the example in this chapter the header records are the ship-to and name-and-address cards, and they are used merely to produce the headings on the invoices being prepared on the printer. In another class of files of this type, the header records are master records, and the detail records are transaction records. For example, the Active Inventory and Sales Deck being fed into the tabulator in Figure 1-17 is an example of such a file. Such files are typically used in punched-card installations and in computer installations in which the only input-output devices on the computer are a card reader, a printer, and a card punch. The deck is prepared for processing by interfiling the detail cards with the master cards on a collator as shown in Figure 1-12. The master file is updated by punching the updated data into previously blank cards.

As an example of how a program to do such updating would be written in RPG language, the following schematic for updating the master file in the simplified inventory application is presented.

1. Two files are described on the File Description Form.
   (a) An input file—the Active Inventory and Sales Deck, to be read on the card reader
   (b) An output file—the Updated Active Inventory Deck, to be punched on the card punch
2. Two record types are described on the Input Form.
   (a) The inventory record, consisting of the stock number and quantity-on-hand fields.
   (b) The sales record, consisting of the stock number and quantity-sold fields.
3. Also indicated on the Input Form is the fact that the stock number field is the control field.
4. When an inventory record is read, no calculation is done, and no output is produced (indicated by the fact that no lines on either the Calculation or Output Forms are conditioned by the record indicator specified for the inventory record on the Input Form).
5. When a sales record is read, the value in the quantity-sold field is subtracted from the value in the quantity-on-hand field, and the resulting value is stored in the quantity-on-hand field (use of the SUB arithmetic operation—subtract factor 2 from factor 1 and store the difference in the result field—on a Calculation Form line conditioned by the record indicator specified for the sales record).
6. When a level break occurs, an updated active inventory record, consisting of the stock number and quantity-on-hand fields, is punched (described on the Output Form).

EXERCISE

A card deck is made up of employee cards and time cards. Employee cards are type 1 cards, time cards are type 2. The deck is in order by employee number. There is one time card for each employee card, which precedes its associated time card in the deck. The layout of the employee card is as follows:

Columns	Fields
1	Type
2–6	Employee number
7–36	Name
37–40	Hourly pay rate in tenths of a cent

The layout of the time card is as follows:

Columns	Fields
1	Type
2–6	Employee number
7, 8, 9	Hours worked in tenths of an hour

The first two digits of the employee number are a department number.

Produce a line item for each employee. On this line, print employee number, name, pay rate, hours worked, and gross pay in appropriately labeled columns. Summarize gross pay by department.

9   MULTIPLE INPUTS

To produce invoices from the input deck described in Chapter 8, a procedure such as that shown in Figure 9-1 would have to be used. The operations shown in Figure 9-1 are analogous to those shown in Figure 1-17, with the computer substituted for the tabulator.

If the computer to be used to produce the invoices were to have two card readers instead of one, the more simple procedure shown in Figure 9-2 could be used. Instead of physically merging the active ship-to and name-and-address cards into the detail deck, the two decks are read from separate readers, and the information is merged inside the computer. Elimination of the physical merge eliminates the necessity for the postprocessing sort and reconstitution of the ship-to and name-and-address deck, since this deck is never dismantled. Both procedures require that both the detail deck and the ship-to and name-and-address deck be in order by customer number.

There are computers available with more than one card reader. The rest of this chapter is devoted to a description of how the RPG might be used to program such a computer to implement the procedure shown in Figure 9-2.

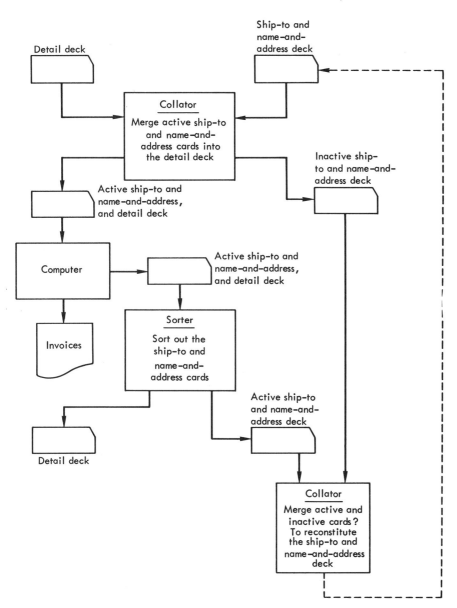

Figure 9-1 Procedure for computer with one card reader.

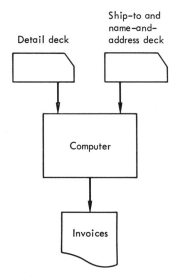

Figure 9-2   Procedure for computer with two card readers.

The input and output files are described on the File Description Form shown in Figure 9-3. The input files are further described on the Input Form shown in Figure 9-4. The specification of the fields on which records from different input files are to be merged is done by making an entry in columns 61 and 62 of the Input Form. Thus, in Figure 9-4 the NAME (ship-to and name-and-address) file and the DETAIL file are merged on the customer number field. The A entered in column 18 of the File Description Form indicates that the

RPG FILE DESCRIPTION FORM

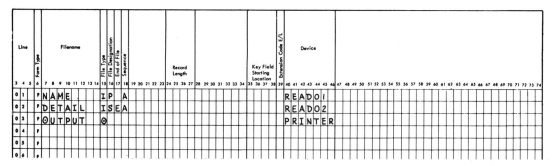

Figure 9-3   Multiple input files.

RPG INPUT FORM

Line	Form Type	Filename	Sequence	Number (1-N)	Option (O)	Record Indicator	Record Identification Codes									Field Location From	To	Decimal Positions	Field Name	Control Level (L1-L9)	Matching Fields or Chaining Fields	Field Indicators Plus	Minus	Zero or Blank
							Position	Not (N)	C/Z/D Character	Position	Not (N)	C/Z/D Character	Position	Not (N)	C/Z/D Character									
01	I	NAME		01	1		01	1		C	1													
02	I															2	8		CUSTA	L1	M1			
03	I															9	28		NAMEA					
04	I															29	48		ADDRA					
05	I															49	68		CITYA					
06	I			02	1		02	1		C	2													
07	I															2	8		CUST	L1	M1			
08	I															9	28		NAME					
09	I															29	48		ADDR					
10	I															49	68		CITY					
11	I	DETAIL					04																	
12	I															2	8		CUST		M1			
13	I															9	14		ITEM					
14	I															15	49		DESC					
15	I															50	53	0	QUANT					
16	I															54	58	2	PRICE					
	I																							
	I																							
	I																							

Figure 9-4 Matching records.

files are in ascending order by customer number and informs the RPG that they are to be merged on that basis.

When the RPG object program finds a record in the DETAIL file with a customer number that matches the customer number of the last processed record in the NAME file, it sets an indicator called the *matching record indicator*. The matching record (MR) indicator remains set as long as a *matching record condition* exists—that is, as long as the current record from the DETAIL file has the same customer number as the last processed NAME record. The MR indicator can be used to condition calculation and output in the same way as the OF, 1P, level, and record indicators.

The entries in column 16 of the File Description Form indicate that the NAME file is the primary (P) file and the DETAIL file is the secondary (S) file. When a matching record condition exists, the RPG object program processes all the primary file records involved in the match before processing any of the secondary file records involved. Thus, in the invoice printing application, when a match is found the ship-to and name-and-address records are processed first, after which the DETAIL records are processed. When the last DETAIL record for a given customer has been processed, the reading of the next record from the NAME file will cause a level break to occur. The MR indicator for this group of customer records remains on during the total time for this level break. Only after this total time is complete will the MR indicator be turned off.

When the last record in the DETAIL file has been processed, then whether or not the last record in the NAME file has been processed, no more invoices are to be produced. As a consequence, the E entered in column 17 of line 2 of Figure 9-3 indicates that when there are no more records in the DETAIL file, total time for the last record can be executed, after which the object program can be brought to a termination.

Specifications for the calculations are shown in Figure 9-5. Lines 1 and 2 of the Calculation Form in this figure indicate that calculations are done during each RPG cycle in which is processed a DETAIL record (record indicator 04 set) that has been matched up with a NAME record (MR indicator set). If a DETAIL record is being processed and the MR indicator is not set, then the DETAIL record must have an erroneous customer number, since it does not match up with any number in the NAME file. Line 3 of Figure 9-5 says that if a DETAIL record is being processed (04 in columns 10 and 11) and its customer number does not match up with any customer number in the NAME file (NMR in columns 12, 13, and 14),

RPG CALCULATION FORM

Line	Form Type	Control Level (L0-L9, LR)	Indicators	Factor 1	Operation	Factor 2	Result Field	Field Length	Decimal Positions	Half Adjust (H)	Resulting Indicators: Plus / Compare High 1>2	Minus / Low 1<2	Zero or Blank / Equal 1=2
01	C		04 MR	QUANT	MULT	PRICE	COST	9	2				
02	C		04 MR	AMT	ADD	COST	AMT	12	2				
03	C		04 NMR		SETON						H1		
04	C												
05	C												
06	C												
07	C												

Figure 9-5 MR indicator use on the calculation form.

RPG OUTPUT DESCRIPTION FORM

Line	Form Type	Filename	Type (H/D/T)	Stacker Select	Space Before	Space After	Skip Before	Skip After	Output Indicators	Field Name	Zero Suppress (Z) / Blank After (B)	End Position in Output Record	Constant or Edit Word
0 1	O	OUTPUT			I		I		02 (MR)				
0 2	O	OR							OFN02				
0 3	O									NAME		40	
0 4	O									NAMEA	B	70	
0 5	O								02	PAGE	Z	83	
0 6	O	OUTPUT			I				02 (MR)				
0 7	O	OR							OFN02				
0 8	O									ADDR		40	
0 9	O									ADDRA	B	70	
1 0	O	OUTPUT					3		02 (MR)				
1 1	O	OR							OFN02				
1 2	O									CITY		40	
1 3	O									CITYA	B	70	
1 4	O	OUTPUT			I				04 N H1				
1 5	O									ITEM		16	
1 6	O									DESC		J3	
1 7	O									QUANT	Z	60	
1 8	O									PRICE		68	' 0. '
1 9	O									COST		83	' , , 0. '
2 0	O	OUTPUT	T				2		L1 N H1 (MR)				
2 1	O									AMT	B	83	' , , , $0. '
	O												
	O												

Figure 9-6 MR indicator use on the output form.

the H1 halt indicator is to be set. Thus, if a DETAIL record with an erroneous customer number is being processed, the H1 indicator is set.

Specifications for the output are shown on the Output Form illustrated in Figure 9-6. The difference between this Output Form and the one shown in Figure 8-8 is the addition of the use of the MR indicator, which is circled in Figure 9-6. Lines 1, 6, and 10 say that a heading is to be produced only if a name-and-address record is being processed (record indicator 2) *and* the MR indicator is set. Line 20 says that a total is to be produced only if level indicator L1 *and* the MR indicator are set. Thus, a name-and-address record whose customer number does not match up with the customer number of any DETAIL record does not produce a heading or a total.

SUMMARY AND ORIENTATION

The new idea introduced in this chapter is the concept of multiple input files. The example in this chapter is for a computer with two card readers (and such computers exist), but when an installation has grown to a size justifying adequate computing power for the use of multiple files as the standard data-processing approach, the physical devices for handling the files are more typically tape handlers. The only impact this change has on the RPG program is in the specification of the devices for the files on the File Description Form.

It is also possible to have multiple output files. This is a matter of describing them on the File Description Form and then specifying on the Output Form the conditions under which records are to be written on these files and the fields of which these records are to consist. Just as input files may be read from card readers, tapes, and disks, so may output files be written on tapes and disks as well as printed or punched on cards. Thus, the use of multiple files as a standard procedure generally marks the departure from card-oriented computer data processing to the use of more powerful peripheral devices such as tape and disk.

The RPG language has now been adequately described so that a program designed to do the fundamental operations required in a sequential data-processing application designed for a tape-oriented computer can be written. The RPG primary input file is typically the input master file, and the secondary file the transaction file.

In light of the above discussion, it may be pointed out that a key characteristic of sequential data processing is the sorting of data, and it may then be asked, "How is a sort written in RPG language?" The answer is that it would be difficult, as it is in any problem-oriented language. The ability to write a sort is typically not built into problem-oriented languages. This is because the computer user typically does not write sorts. Generalized sort programs are written by computer manufacturers, these sort programs are supplied at no extra cost to their customers, and it is these sorts that users employ to sort their data.

EXERCISE

An employee card deck is read through one reader, a time-card deck through a second reader. Both decks are in order by employee number. There is a one-to-one correspondence between employee and time cards. The layout of the employee card is as follows:

Columns	Fields
2–6	Employee number
7–36	Name
37–40	Hourly pay rate in tenths of a cent

The layout of the time card is as follows:

Columns	Fields
2–6	Employee number
7, 8, 9	Hours worked in tenths of an hour

The first two digits of the employee number are a department number.

Produce a line item for each employee. On this line, print employee number, name, pay rate, hours worked, and gross pay in appropriately labeled columns. Summarize gross pay by department.

10 TABLES

To get the PRICE field punched into a DETAIL card, it is necessary to locate the item number of the item sold in a price list, look up the price given in the price list for that item, and keypunch the price into the card. If the price list (or price *table*) were present in the computer's memory, none of this preparation would be required. Instead, the computer could be used to look up the pertinent price in the table as each DETAIL record is processed.

Thus, suppose the DETAIL card has the format shown in Figure 10-1. This DETAIL card has the same format as the DETAIL card shown in Figure 6-1 except that the price field is no longer present.

Also, suppose we have a deck of cards of the format shown in Figure 10-2, where each price field contains the price for the item whose number immediately precedes it in the card.

Finally, suppose the supplier doing the invoicing carries a line of 98 different items. That is, there are 98 entries in the price table. Thus, the price table consists of 14 cards. The remainder of this chapter is devoted to a description of how the RPG might be used to produce invoices with the use of a price table.

The file description is shown on the File Description Form

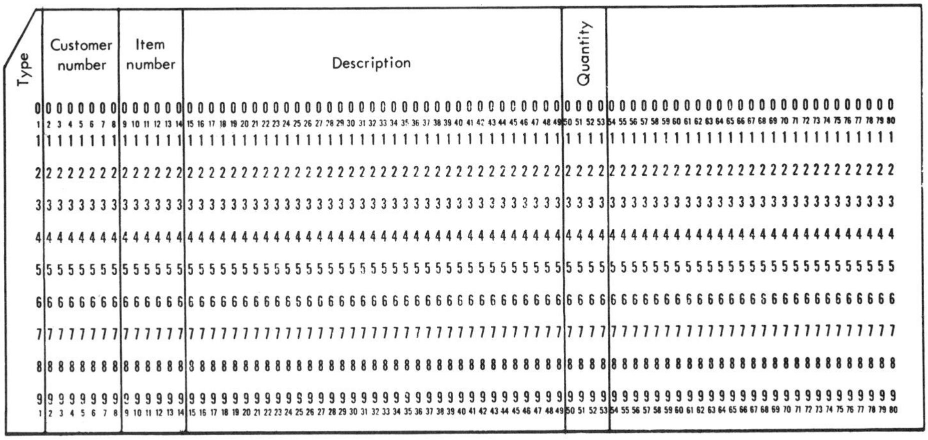

Figure 10-1 Detail card.

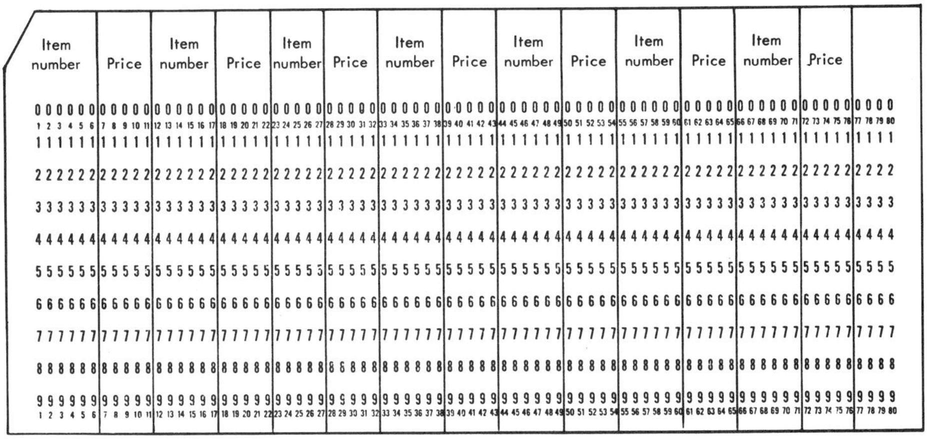

Figure 10-2 Price table card.

illustrated in Figure 10-3. The price table is described as the PRICE file on the first line of the File Description Form. It is an input file (I in column 15), but instead of being a primary or secondary file, it is a *table file* (T in column 16). The PRICE file is read from reader 1, the same device from which the NAME file is read. No confusion results here, since the RPG object program reads the whole table and stores it in memory before starting the processing opera-

RPG FILE DESCRIPTION FORM

Line	Form Type	Filename	File Type	File Designation	End of File	Sequence			Record Length		Key Field Starting Location	Extension Code E/L	Device	
0 1	F	PRICE	I	T								E	READ01	
0 2	F	NAME	I	P		A							READ01	
0 3	F	DETAIL	I	S	E	A							READ02	
0 4	F	OUTPUT	O										PRINTER	
0 5	F													

Figure 10-3 Table input.

tion shown in Figure 7-7. The E in column 39 indicates that the
PRICE file is described in greater detail on the *File Extension Form*.
There is no change in the description of the NAME, DETAIL, and
OUTPUT files shown on lines 2, 3, and 4 of Figure 10-3.

The File Extension Form information for the PRICE file is
shown in Figure 10-4. This information says that the name of the
file is PRICE (columns 11 through 18), that the file has 98 entries
(98 in columns 36 through 39), that seven entries appear in each
PRICE file record (7 in columns 33, 34, and 35), that the first
field in an entry is the item number field TABITM in columns 27
through 32), and that the second field in an entry is the price field
(TABPRC in columns 46 through 51). This information also says
that the item number field is an alphabetic field (no entry in column
44) containing six characters (6 in columns 40, 41, and 42), and

RPG FILE EXTENSION FORM

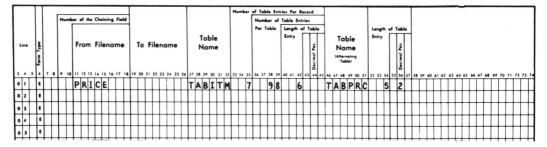

Figure 10-4 File extension.

RPG INPUT FORM

Line	Form Type	Filename	Sequence	Number (1-N)	Option (O)	Resulting Indicator	Position	Not (N) / C/Z/D / Character	Position	Not (N) / C/Z/D / Character	Position	Not (N) / C/Z/D / Character	From	To	Decimal Positions	Field Name	Control Level (L1-L9)	Matching Fields or Chaining Fields	Plus	Minus	Zero or Blank
01	I	NAME	01	1	0	01	1	C 1													
02	I												2	8		CUSTA		LIM1			
03	I												9	28		NAMEA					
04	I												29	48		ADDRA					
05	I												49	68		CITYA					
06	I		02	1		02	1	C2													
07	I												2	8		CUST		LIM1			
08	I												9	28		NAME					
09	I												29	48		ADDR					
10	I												49	68		CITY					
11	I	DETAIL				04															
12	I												2	8		CUST		M1			
13	I												9	14		ITEM					
14	I												15	49		DESC					
15	I												50	53	0	QUANT					

Figure 10-5 Input to table lookup.

that the price field is a numeric field five digits in length (5 in columns 52, 53, and 54) with a decimal point two digits in from the right (2 in column 56).

RPG CALCULATION FORM

Line	Form Type	Control Level (L0-L9, LR)	Indicators Not	And Not	And Not	Factor 1	Operation	Factor 2	Result Field	Field Length	Decimal Positions	Half Adjust (H)	High 1>2	Low 1<2	Equal 1=2	Plus	Minus	Zero or Blank
01	C		04	MR		ITEM	LOKUP	TABITM	TABPRC						10			
02	C		10			QUANT	MULT	TABPRC	COST	9	2							
03	C		10			AMT	ADD	COST	AMT	12	2							
04	C		04	NMR			SETON						H1					
05	C		N10				SETON						H2					
06	C																	
07	C																	

Figure 10-6 Table lookup.

The NAME and DETAIL input files are further described on the Input Form shown in Figure 10-5. The only difference between this description and the one shown in Figure 9-4 is that the DETAIL record no longer contains a price field.

The calculations necessary to produce the invoices are described on the Calculation Form shown in Figure 10-6. Line 1 of Figure 10-6 says that the value of the item field of the current DETAIL record is to be compared against the item number field of the price table entries. If an entry is found with an item number equal to the ITEM value, the price field of that entry is to subsequently be used whenever the price field is referenced. If any entry is found with an item number equal to the ITEM value, the resulting indicator number 10 is set. If no such entry is found, resulting indicator 10 is reset.

RPG OUTPUT DESCRIPTION FORM

Line	Form Type	Filename	Type (H/D/T)	Stacker Select	Space Before	Space After	Skip Before	Skip After	Output Indicators	And	And	Field Name	Zero Suppress (Z)	Blank After (B)	End Position in Output Record	Constant or Edit Word
01	O	OUTPUT				1	1		02	MR						
02	O		OR						OF	N02						
03	O											NAME			40	
04	O											NAMEA		B	70	
05	O								02			PAGE	Z		83	
06	O	OUTPUT				1			02	MR						
07	O		OR						OF	N02						
08	O											ADDR			40	
09	O											ADDRA		B	70	
10	O	OUTPUT						3	02	MR						
11	O		OR						OF	N02						
12	O											CITY			40	
13	O											CITYA		B	70	
14	O	OUTPUT				1			04	NH1	NH2					
15	O											ITEM			16	
16	O											DESC			53	
17	O											QUANT	Z		60	
18	O											TABPRC			68	' 0. '
19	O											COST			83	' , , 0. '
20	O	OUTPUT	T				2		LI	NH1	MR					
21	O		AND						NH2							
22	O											AMT		B	83	' , , $0. '
	O															
	O															

Figure 10-7 Output form table lookup.

Lines 2, 3, and 4 of Figure 10-6 specify the invoice calculations with which we are familiar. However, lines 2 and 3 specify that the calculations are to be done only if resulting indicator 10 is set (no error has occurred). Thus, calculations are not performed in an error situation.

Line 5 says that if a DETAIL record contains an ITEM field value not present in the price table (resulting indicator 10 reset), the H2 halt indicator is to be set. Consequently, under such an error condition, program execution is not allowed to continue. The conditions under which an RPG object program ceases execution vary depending on whether the H1 or the H2 indicator caused the cessation. Thus, if the program terminates with an error situation, it can be determined from the nature of the terminating conditions whether a DETAIL record has an erroneous customer number or ITEM number.

To exemplify the way in which table lookup works, consider the partial listing of the price table given in Table 10-1. If a DETAIL record with an item number field containing 011434 is currently being processed, then the lookup of

ITEM   LOKUP   TABITM   TABPRC

Table 10-1

Item number	Price
011426	$3.67
011428	0.99
011430	5.37
011432	2.64
011434	7.80
011436	7.20
011438	9.86
011440	4.85
011442	10.79
011444	6.25
011446	5.87
011448	6.30
011450	1.42

would select and make available for use in subsequent processing the price of $7.80. The subsequent calculation

QUANT   MULT   TABPRC   COST

would produce a COST that is the result of multiplying the current quantity value by $7.80. If on the other hand the current DETAIL record has an item number of 011442, the multiplication would be by the price $10.79.

Output specifications to produce the invoices are shown in Figure 10-7. The only difference between this Output Form and the one shown in Figure 9-6 is the use of the H2 indicator to prevent the production of output by an erroneous DETAIL record. This use of the H2 indicator is shown in the circled portion of Figure 10-7.

The total output is now conditioned by the state of four different indicators: L1, NH1, MR, and NH2. Lines 20 and 21 of Figure 10-7 show how this type of AND condition is written.

SUMMARY AND ORIENTATION

The use of the table in the above example simplifies the work required to do the processing—no prior step, mechanized or manual, is required to get the price value in each DETAIL card. Such is typical of the use of tables, a programming technique that involves keeping track of information in the computer's memory during processing rather than trying to handle the information as some kind of external sequential file. The example given here shows how a table can be used to supply to a program information that would otherwise have to be fed in by some form of input. Tables are also used as a series of slots in which to summarize information that would otherwise have to be produced as output, sorted into the categories by which it is to be summarized, and then once more introduced as input for summary purposes. Thus, it can be seen that, to the limited extent to which restrictions on memory size make their use practical, tables are a device used to make possible the processing of data in random sequence. For example, in the above illustration, DETAIL records are being processed in customer number order. Therefore, the item numbers, on the basis of which the prices are accessed, occur randomly. Similarly, information that is being summarized into categories other than the ones in which the data is inputted for processing is being processed randomly.

EXERCISE

An employee card deck is read through one reader, a time-card deck through a second reader. Both decks are in order by employee number. There is a one-to-one correspondence between employee and time cards. The layout of the employee card is as follows:

Columns	Fields
2–6	Employee Number
7–36	Name

The layout of the time card is as follows:

Columns	Fields
2–6	Employee Number
7, 8, 9	Hours worked in tenths of an hour

The first two digits of the employee number are a department number.

Preceding the employee cards in the first reader is a card whose first 78 columns are divided into 13 groups of 6 columns each. Within each group of 6 columns, the first 2 columns hold a department number, and the last 4 hold the pay rate (in tenths of a cent) for the people who work in the department with the associated number.

Produce a line item for each employee. On this line, print employee number, name, pay rate, hours worked, and gross pay in appropriately labeled columns. Summarize gross pay by department.

11 RANDOM ACCESS

A file on a random access device is not functionally different from a table stored in memory. As indicated in the last chapter, a table is just a type of file in which the program desires to look things up, that is, which the program desires to access randomly. If all of a user's tables or random access files were small enough to fit in memory, he would never have the desire to use a random access device. It is only because the cost of a random access device is small relative to the cost of memory that the user with large random access files turns to the use of such a device. Thus, suppose our supplier who is using the computer to do his invoicing has such a large line that he cannot fit his price table or price file in memory. The rest of this chapter is devoted to a description of how the RPG might be used to program a computer in the production of invoices when the price file is recorded on a random access device.

The characteristics of a random access file are described below by analogy to a table. A random access file consists of a number of entries, as does a table. However, in the case of a random access file each entry is called a record. Each random access file record has a key field, on the basis of which the program looks up information in the file in a manner similar to the way it looks up information in a table. In the RPG, this key is called the *chaining field*.

In the RPG, a random access file is called a *chained file*. The price file is therefore a chained file. The file that is processed against the chained file is called the *chaining file*. Thus, the DETAIL file is the chaining file to the price file. Both the chaining file and the chained file contain the chaining key. Therefore, both the DETAIL file and the price file contain the item number field, the field on the basis of which an appropriate price file record is matched up with a given DETAIL file record.

When the RPG object program prepares to process a chaining file record, it first looks up and makes available for processing the appropriate chained file record. For example, when the object program prepares to process a DETAIL file record, it looks up and makes available the price file record with the corresponding item number. The program can detect whether or not a price file record corresponding to the current DETAIL record has been located, because the price file record indicator will be set when the location has been made and reset when the search has failed.

Some random access devices are *character oriented*. That is, a record may begin in any character position on the device and may extend for as many characters as desired, after which another record begins. For example, a price file record consists of a six-position item number field and a five-position price field. As a consequence, each record in the price file can be 11 positions long and can be packed one after the other on the random access device. The item number field appears in positions 1 through 6 of the price file record and the price field in positions 7 through 11.

The input and output files for our random access application are described on the File Description Form shown in Figure 11-1. The PRICE file is an input file, but instead of being a primary, secondary, or table file, it is a chained file (C in column 16). The PRICE file is recorded on a random access device, in this case, a disk (DISK in columns 40 through 46). Each record in the PRICE file is 11 positions long (11 in columns 24 through 27), and the item number field (the chaining field) begins in position 1 of the record (1 in columns 35 through 38). The only change to the description of the NAME, DETAIL, and OUTPUT files is the entry of an E in

RPG FILE DESCRIPTION FORM

Line	Form Type	Filename	File Type	File Designation	End of File	Sequence	Record Length	Key Field Starting Location	Extension Code E/L	Device	
0 1	F	P R I C E	I C				1 1		I	D I S K	
0 2	F	N A M E	I P	A						R E A D 0 1	
0 3	F	D E T A I L	I S E	A					E	R E A D 0 2	
0 4	F	O U T P U T	O							P R I N T E R	
0 5	F										
0 6	F										

Figure 11-1   Random access input.

column 39 for the DETAIL file, which indicates that the DETAIL file is described in greater detail on the File Extension Form.

The file extension information for the DETAIL file is shown on the File Extension Form in Figure 11-2. This information says that the DETAIL file is the chaining file (DETAIL in columns 11 through 18), that the file to which the DETAIL file is chained is the PRICE file (PRICE in columns 19 through 26), and that the chaining field which chains these two files together will be identified by the *chaining flag* C1 in the description of the chaining file (in this case, the DETAIL file) on the Input Form.

The NAME, DETAIL, and PRICE files are described further on the Input Form shown in Figure 11-3. The PRICE file is described on lines 11, 12, and 13. Line 11 says that when a PRICE file record with the same item number as the current DETAIL file record is located, record indicator 03 is to be set (03 in columns 19 and 20). Lines

RPG FILE EXTENSION FORM

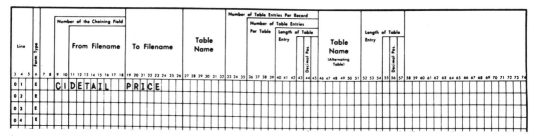

Line	Form Type	Number of the Chaining Field	From Filename	To Filename	Table Name	Number of Table Entries Per Record	Number of Table Entries Per Table	Length of Table Entry	Decimal Pos.	Table Name (Alternating Table)	Length of Table Entry	Decimal Pos.	
0 1	E	C 1	D E T A I L	P R I C E									
0 2	E												
0 3	E												
0 4	E												

Figure 11-2   Chaining file extension.

RPG INPUT FORM

Line	Form Type	Filename	Sequence	Number (1-N)	Option (O)	Resulting Indicator	Position 1	Not (N)	C/Z/D	Character	Position 2	Not (N)	C/Z/D	Character	Position 3	Not (N)	C/Z/D	Character	From	To	Decimal Positions	Field Name	Control Level (1-9)	Matching Fields or Chaining Fields	Plus	Minus	Zero or Blank
01	I	NAME	01	1	0	01	1		C	1																	
02	I																		2	8		CUSTA			L	I	M I
03	I																		9	28		NAMEA					
04	I																		29	48		ADDRA					
05	I																		49	68		CITYA					
06	I		02	1		02	1		C	2																	
07	I																		2	8		CUST			L	I	M I
08	I																		9	28		NAME					
09	I																		29	48		ADDR					
10	I																		49	68		CITY					
11	I	PRICE				03																					
12	I																		1	6		ITEMNO					
13	I																		7	11	2	PRICE					
14	I	DETAIL				04																					
15	I																		2	8		CUST			M I		
16	I																		9	14		ITEM			C I		
17	I																		15	49		DESC					
18	I																		50	53	0	QUANT					

Figure 11-3 Random access input.

12 and 13 describe the fields making up a record in the PRICE file.

The description of the NAME and DETAIL files is the same as before with the single addition that the ITEM field of the DETAIL file

RPG CALCULATION FORM

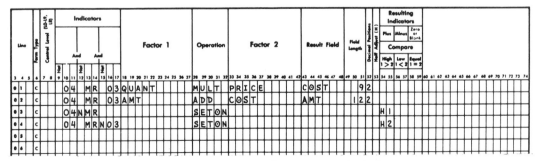

Figure 11-4 Random access calculation.

is identified as the chaining field. This identification is made by means of the entry of the chaining flag defined on the File Extension Form (C1 in columns 61 and 62 of line 16).

The calculations necessary to produce the invoices are described on the Calculation Form shown in Figure 11-4. Lines 1, 2, and 3 of Figure 11-4 specify the invoice calculations with which we are familiar. However, lines 1 and 2 specify that the calculations are to be done only if record indicator 4 and the MR indicator are set (a DETAIL record with a matching customer number is being processed) and record indicator 3 is set (a PRICE record with an item number field value equal to the ITEM field value of the DETAIL record has been located and made available for processing). Thus, the appropriate PRICE is available for the calculations.

Line 4 says that if a DETAIL record with a matching customer number is being processed (04 in columns 10 and 11 and MR in columns 13 and 14) and no PRICE record has been located with an item number field value equal to the ITEM field value of the DETAIL record (N03 in columns 15, 16, and 17), the H2 halt indicator is to be set. Thus, if a DETAIL record with an erroneous item number field is being processed, the H2 indicator will be set, and no calculations will be done.

The output specifications in the Output Form shown in Figure 10-7 can be used to produce the invoices.

SUMMARY AND ORIENTATION

In a batch-processing environment the use of random access devices is restricted to the processing of large tables as illustrated above. In general, it is difficult to justify the installation of random access devices and, consequently, the use of random data processing in a batch-processing environment. Applications are more typically tape oriented and sequential in nature.

To justify random access equipment a need for realtime data processing has to be established. Then random access processing becomes imperative, since transactions that are processed on a realtime basis will occur in a random order as far as any matching key is concerned.

The RPG language as it is presently implemented does not have the facility for realtime data processing. However, if we know how an RPG object program is executed, we can extend this knowledge to conceive of the operation of a realtime program. The basic cycle of an RPG object program is to read an input record, process it, go back and read the next input record, process it, and so on, continuing in this loop until there are no more input records. For example, if in the above illustration all other operations are ignored, the program can be conceived of as a loop in which the next DETAIL record is read, after which an access is made to the PRICE file on the basis of ITEM number to determine the price to be associated with the item described by the current DETAIL record. The existence of the loop identifies the program as a batch operation—it is designed to process a batch of DETAIL records.

The essential difference in structure between a batch and a realtime program is that after processing the current DETAIL record, instead of looping back to read the next DETAIL record as does the batch program, the realtime program "waits" until an interrupt occurs. This interrupt indicates that another DETAIL record, or inquiry for an item price, is ready to be processed, at which point it will then "loop back," process the inquiry, and then once more enter the "wait state." This "waiting" is generally done by *releasing* "control" (the ability to execute instructions) to the *operating system*, a kind of super program under whose "supervision" the realtime program is executed. The operating system finds other things for the computer to do while waiting for the next inquiry. The arrival of the inquiry will be signalled by an interrupt, at which point the operating system passes control to the realtime program so it can process the inquiry. A schematic that shows this structural difference between a batch and a realtime program is shown in Figure 11-5.

It is difficult to conceive of the practicality of a PRICE file stored on a random access device with a realtime computer system being used to inquire as to item prices. However, for example, for large-scale inventory applications it is practical to

1. Have the inventory file stored on a random access device.
2. Have a realtime computer system that

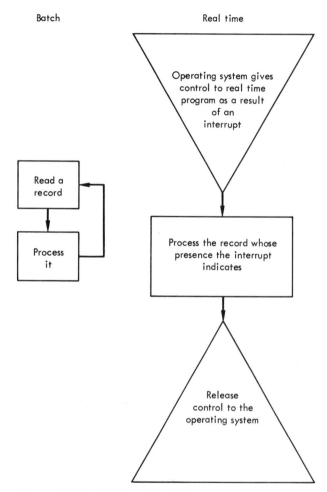

Batch   Real time

Figure 11-5   Batch and real time program structure.

(a) Looks up stock levels as a result of inquiries.
(b) Reduces stock levels as a result of sales.

Specifically, airlines use such a system to inquire as to seat availability on specified flights and to remove space from the available list when seats are booked.

EXERCISE

An employee card deck is read through one reader, a time-card deck through a second reader. Both decks are in order by employee number. There is a one-to-one correspondence between employee and time cards. The layout of the employee card is as follows:

Columns	Fields
2–6	Employee number
7–26	Name

The layout of the time card is as follows:

Columns	Fields
2–6	Employee number
7, 8, 9	Hours worked in tenths of an hour

The first two digits of the employee number are a department number.

A pay rate file is recorded on a disk. Each record in the pay-rate file is 6 positions long. The first 2 positions contain a department number, and the last 4 contain the pay rate (in tenths of a cent) for the people who work in the department with the associated number.

Produce a line item for each employee. On this line, print employee number, name, pay rate, hours worked, and gross pay in appropriately labeled columns. Summarize gross pay by department.

12 LEVELS OF CONTROL

In the invoice example used previously in this book only one level of control was employed. More than one level of control is available in RPG programs, and to illustrate their use the following example is presented.

Suppose we have a deck of cards with the format shown in Figure 12-1. This deck constitutes a detail labor file. Each card in the deck is a record identifying an employee by name and employee number, specifying by number in what department and division he works, and stating that this employee worked a given number of hours. There can be more than one record in the file for a given employee.

The records are in order in the file first by division number, then by department number, and finally by employee number. Thus, the file is organized on three levels. The highest level of organization is by division number. All records with the same division number are grouped together in the file with a *break* of division number between groups. The next level of organization is by department number. A group of records all with the same division number is itself organized into a number of groups, all records in such a sub-

Div #	Dept #	Emp #	Employee name	Hours wkd	

```
0000 0000 000000 00000000000000000 00000 000000000000000000000000000000000000000000000000000000
1 2 3 4 5 6 7 8 9 10 11 12 13 14 15 16 17 18 19 20 21 22 23 24 25 26 27 28 29 30 31 32 33 34 35 36 37 38 39 40 41 42 43 44 45 46 47 48 49 50 51 52 53 54 55 56 57 58 59 60 61 62 63 64 65 66 67 68 69 70 71 72 73 74 75 76 77 78 79 80
1111 1111 111111 11111111111111111 11111 111111111111111111111111111111111111111111111111111111
2222 2222 222222 22222222222222222 22222 222222222222222222222222222222222222222222222222222222
3333 3333 333333 33333333333333333 33333 333333333333333333333333333333333333333333333333333333
4444 4444 444444 44444444444444444 44444 444444444444444444444444444444444444444444444444444444
5555 5555 555555 55555555555555555 55555 555555555555555555555555555555555555555555555555555555
6666 6666 666666 66666666666666666 66666 666666666666666666666666666666666666666666666666666666
7777 7777 777777 77777777777777777 77777 777777777777777777777777777777777777777777777777777777
8888 8888 888888 88888888888888888 88888 888888888888888888888888888888888888888888888888888888
9999 9999 999999 99999999999999999 99999 999999999999999999999999999999999999999999999999999999
1 2 3 4 5 6 7 8 9 10 11 12 13 14 15 16 17 18 19 20 21 22 23 24 25 26 27 28 29 30 31 32 33 34 35 36 37 38 39 40 41 42 43 44 45 46 47 48 49 50 51 52 53 54 55 56 57 58 59 60 61 62 63 64 65 66 67 68 69 70 71 72 73 74 75 76 77 78 79 80
```

Figure 12-1 Detail labor card.

group having the same department number. The lowest level of organization is by employee number. In each group of records with a common combined division-department number, the records are broken into subgroups by employee number.

The information on the Input Form shown in Figure 12-2 describes the detail labor file. As shown on this form, the lowest level control field is the employee number field and is assigned the level break indicator L1. The next higher level control field is department number and is assigned level break indicator L2. The

RPG INPUT FORM

Line	Form Type	Filename	Sequence	Number (1-N) Option (O)	Resulting Indicator	Record Identification Codes										Field Location			Field Name	Control Level (L1-L9)	Matching Fields or Chaining Fields	Field Indicators		
						Position	Not (N)	C/Z/D	Character	Position	Not (N)	C/Z/D	Character	Position	Not (N)	C/Z/D	Character	From	To	Decimal Positions			Plus	Minus	Zero or Blank
0 1	I	LABOR																							
0 2	I																	1	4		DIV	L3		
0 3	I																	5	8		DEPT	L2		
0 4	I																	9	14		EMPNO	L1		
0 5	I																	15	28		NAME			
0 6	I																	29	33	0	HOURS			
0 7	I																							
0 8	I																							

Figure 12-2 Multiple level breaks.

highest level control field is division number and is assigned level break indicator L3. Thus, the higher the control field level, the larger the number of the level break indicator assigned to it.

Level break indicators have the property that, whenever one is set, all lower numbered level break indicators are also set. Thus, if a control break occurs that results in the setting of level break indicator L2, level break indicator L1 is also set. This means that when a control break occurs on a certain level, a control break at all lower levels automatically results. Thus, a break in department number implies a break in employee number, and a break in division number implies a break in department and employee number.

Suppose that from the LABOR file it is desired to print a report like the one shown in Figure 12-3. This particular report says that Smith, whose employee number is 011426, works in department number 0246, which is in division 0112, and has three records in the LABOR file, one for 101 hours, one for 100 hours, and one for 102 hours, for a total of 303 hours. Jones also works in department 0246, division 0112, and has two records in the LABOR file for a total of 242 hours. And so on. Smith, Jones, and Brown make up the department numbered 0246, and a total of 748 hours was worked by this department. Division number 0112 is made up of departments 0246 and 0310, and 1317 hours were worked by this division. The records for two divisions are present in the LABOR file, and a grand total of 2402 hours was worked. The level of each total is indicated on the report by the number of asterisks that are printed after the number.

The calculations required to produce the Labor Summarization shown in Figure 12-3 are shown on the Calculation Form in Figure 12-4. If a Calculation Form line has an entry in columns 7 and 8, the calculation described on that line is done at total time. All entries in columns 7 and 8 are level break indicators, and the line is done at total time only if the level break indicator specified in columns 7 and 8 is set. Thus, line 1 of Figure 12-4 says that at each detail time the HOURS from the LABOR record are to be added to an employee total. Line 2 says that when a break occurs on employee number, then at total time the employee total is to be added into a department total. Line 3 says that when a break occurs on department number, then at total time the department total is to be added into a division

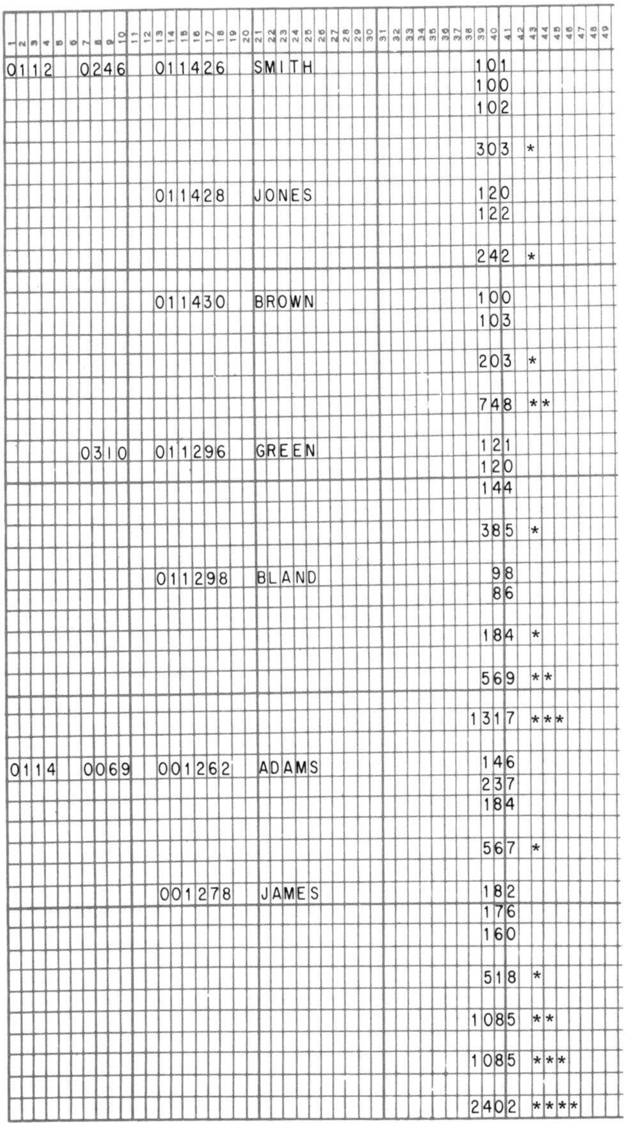

Figure 12-3 Group-indicated labor summarization.

total. Line 4 says that when a break occurs on division number, then at total time the division total is to be added into a grand total.

The output specifications required to produce the Labor Sum-

RPG CALCULATION FORM

Line	Form Type	Control Level (L0-L9, LR)	Indicators And Not	And Not	And Not	Factor 1	Operation	Factor 2	Result Field	Field Length	Decimal Positions	Half Adjust (H)	Resulting Indicators Plus	Minus	Zero or Blank Compare High 1>2	Low 1<2	Equal 1=2	
0 1	C					EMPTOT	ADD	HOURS	EMPTOT	7 0								
0 2	C	L 1				DEPTOT	ADD	EMPTOT	DEPTOT	8 0								
0 3	C	L 2				DIVTOT	ADD	DEPTOT	DIVTOT	8 0								
0 4	C	L 3				GRNTOT	ADD	DIVTOT	GRNTOT	8 0								
0 5	C																	

Figure 12-4 Multiple level summarization.

marization are shown on the Output Form in Figure 12-5. There are two new items on this Output Form.

1. One of these is the use of the *last record indicator*, written as LR. As indicated in Figure 7-7, the LR indicator is set when there are no more input records. It can be used to condition calculations and output in the same way as the

RPG OUTPUT DESCRIPTION FORM

Line	Form Type	Filename	Type (H/D/T)	Stacker Select	Space Before	After	Skip Before	After	Output Indicators And Not	And Not	And Not	Field Name	Zero Suppress (Z)	Blank After (B)	End Position in Output Record	Constant or Edit Word
0 1	O	OUTPUT			1											
0 2	O								L3			DIV			4	
0 3	O								L2			DEPT			1 0	
0 4	O								L1			EMPNO			1 8	
0 5	O								L1			NAME			3 4	
0 6	O											HOURS	Z		4 1	
0 7	O	OUTPUT	T	1 2					L1							
0 8	O											EMPTOT	B		4 3	' 0 &* '
0 9	O	OUTPUT	T	2					L2							
1 0	O											DEPTOT	B		4 4	' 0 &** '
1 1	O	OUTPUT	T	2					L3							
1 2	O											DIVTOT	B		4 5	' 0 &*** '
1 3	O	OUTPUT	T						LR							
1 4	O											GRNTOT			4 6	' 0 &**** '
1 5	O															

Figure 12-5 Multiple level output.

OF, 1P, level, record, MR, and resulting indicators, as is done on line 13.

2. The other new item consists of the ampersands and asterisks in the edit word.

   (a) Whenever an ampersand appears in an edit word a space appears in the printed output.

   (b) An edit word may end with one or more asterisks. They appear unchanged in the printed output.

EXERCISE

Given a deck of cards with the following layout:

Columns	Fields
1–4	County number
5–8	Town number
9–12	District number
13–20	Tax dollars collected in cents

The deck is in order first by county number, then by town number, and finally by district number. Print a summary report of taxes collected. The report is to contain a grand total; subtotals for each county; and within each county, subtotals for each town.

13 UPDATED TABLES

In Chapter 10 an example was given of the use of a table as input to a program. An input table can also be updated and produced as output from a program.

For example, suppose that we have the LABOR file used to produce the Labor Summarization but that the records in the file are no longer in order by division number. Also, suppose the company for whom the Labor Summarization was made consists of 30 different divisions. Finally, suppose we want to produce a deck of five cards, each of the format shown in Figure 13-1. This deck of cards makes up a summary table. Each division number field of the summary table is to contain the number of a division of the company, and each total-hours field is to contain the total hours worked in the division whose number is in the preceding division number field. The remainder of this chapter is devoted to a description of how the RPG might be used to produce such a summary deck.

To produce such a summary table deck as output, a similar summary table deck must be read in as input. This input summary table deck would have a division number in each division number field, but all total-hours fields must contain zeros.

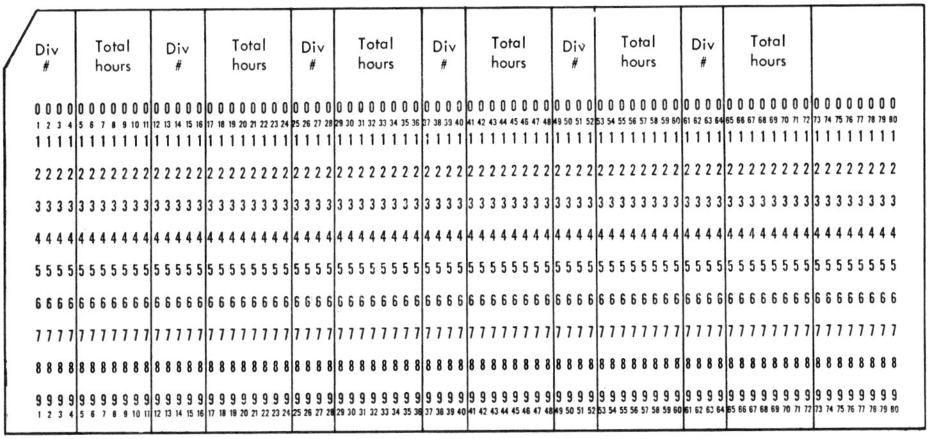

Figure 13-1 Summary table card.

The file description for this summary operation is shown on the File Description Form in Figure 13-2. Both lines 1 and 3 describe the summary table. Line 1 describes the summary table as an input file; line 3 as an output file. The RPG object program reads the summary table from the card reader and stores it in memory before processing begins. Then after all processing is finished (the LR indicator has been set and total time completed), the RPG object program punches the summary table into a deck of blank cards on the punch.

The File Extension Form information for the TABLE file is shown in Figure 13-3. The entry in columns 19 through 26 specifies that after the TABLE file has been read in and processed, it is to be produced as the output file named SUMMARY.

RPG FILE DESCRIPTION FORM

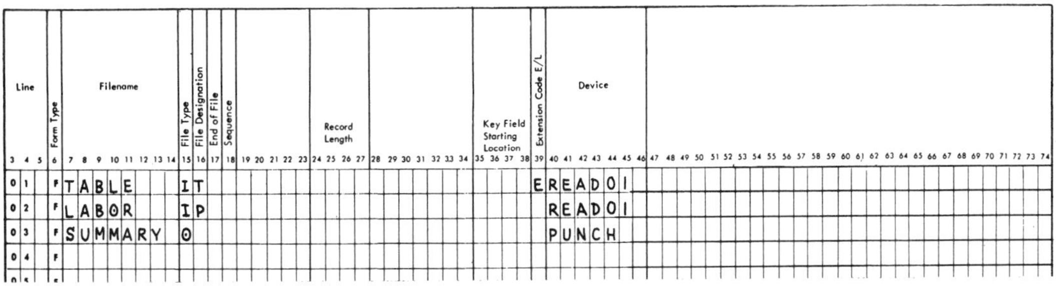

Figure 13-2 Table output.

RPG FILE EXTENSION FORM

Line	Form Type	Number of the Chaining Field	From Filename	To Filename	Table Name	Number of Table Entries Per Record				Table Name (Alternating Table)	Length of Table Entry		
						Number of Table Entries Per Table	Length of Table Entry						
01	E		TABLE	SUMMARY	TABDIV	6	30	4		TABTOT	8	0	
02	E												
03	E												
04	E												

Figure 13-3   File extension for table output.

The description of the LABOR file shown on the Input Form in Figure 12-2 is sufficient for the production of the summary table deck. The necessary calculations are described on the Calculation Form shown in Figure 13-4. Line 1 of this figure says that if a summary table entry is found with a division number field having a value equal to the value of the division number field of the current LABOR record, then the total field of that summary table entry is to subsequently be used whenever the TABTOT field is referenced. Line 2 says that if such a find has occurred, the HOURS field of the current LABOR record is to be added to the total field so located. In this way, as the LABOR file records are processed, the hours worked are accumulated by division in the summary table.

RPG CALCULATION FORM

Line	Form Type	Control Level	Indicators			Factor 1	Operation	Factor 2	Result Field	Field Length	Decimal Positions	Resulting Indicators		
			And	And								Plus / Minus / Zero or Blank	High / Low / Equal	
01	C					DIV	LOKUP	TABDIV	TABTOT			10		
02	C		10			TABTOT	ADD	HOURS	TABTOT					
03	C		N10				SETON					H1		
04	C													
05	C													
06	C													

Figure 13-4   Calculations for table output.

The only output to this program is the summary table deck. Consequently, no Output Form needs to be supplied.

EXERCISE

Given a deck of cards with the following layout:

Columns	Fields
1–4	County number
5–8	Town number
9–12	District number
13–20	Tax dollars collected in cents

The deck is in random order. Produce a card deck that contains a total tax monies collected in each county and that identifies each total by county number. There are 42 counties in the state.

14 CALCULATIONS

The preceding examples have used only a limited amount of the calculation power available in the RPG. So far, the only calculation operations used in this book have been multiply (MULT), add (ADD), subtract (SUB), table lookup (LOKUP), and setting an indicator (SETON). There are several other calculation operations available in RPG language. Besides addition, subtraction, and multiplication, the arithmetic operation of division (DIV—divide factor 1 by factor 2 and store the quotient in the result) is provided.

During all arithmetic operations the RPG object program automatically handles all decimal alignment. For example, for the operation described on line 1 of the Calculation Form in Figure 14-1, if the field MIN has a value of 98765432 and a decimal point three places in from the right, and the field SUBTRA has a value of 123456739 and a decimal point four places in from the right, then as the result of the subtraction operation a value of 8641975 is stored in the field DIFF.

It should be noted that the RPG object program automatically truncates result values to fit them into the specified result fields. For

RPG CALCULATION FORM

Line	Form Type	Control Level	Indicators	Factor 1	Operation	Factor 2	Result Field	Field Length	Decimal Positions	Half Adjust (H)	Resulting Indicators
01	C			MIN	SUB	SUBTRA	DIFF	72			
02	C			MIN	SUB	SUBTRA	DIFF	72		H	71 51 6
03	C			A	COMP	B					30 32 31
04	C			SEX	COMP	'M'					55 55 50
05	C			CLAIM	SUB	50.00	PAYMNT	72			
06	C				MOVE	ORIG	DEST	5			
07	C				SETON						OF 60 70
08	C				SETOF						MR 80
09	C										

Figure 14-1   Calculations.

example, in the preceding subtraction example, the subtraction specified is as follows.

$$98765.4320$$
$$-12345.6739$$
$$\overline{86419.7581}$$

However, since DIFF is described as a seven-position field with a decimal point two places in from the right, the last two digits of the difference are truncated before it is stored in DIFF.

A result that is to be truncated can be rounded, or *half-adjusted*, before truncation if such an operation is specified. For example, given the same field values and characteristics, the operation described on line 2 of Figure 14-1 would cause a value of 8641976 to be stored in DIFF. In this case, the steps performed before the truncation are as follows.

$$98765.4320$$
$$-12345.6739$$
$$\overline{86419.7581}$$
$$+00000.0050$$
$$\overline{86419.7631}$$

As shown on line 2 of Figure 14-1, halfadjustment is specified by placing an H in column 53 of the Calculation Form line on which is described the operation the result of which is to be halfadjusted.

Resulting indicators can be set as a consequence of an arithmetic operation. A resulting indicator can be set if a result value is less than zero, equal to zero, or more than zero. For example, for line 2 of Figure 14-1, indicator 15 is set if DIFF turns out to be less than zero, indicator 16 is set if DIFF is equal to zero, and 17 is set if DIFF is more than zero. If a resulting indicator is specified and the conditions for setting the indicator are not met, then the indicator is reset. For example, if the value of DIFF turns out to be 8641976, then indicator 17 is set ,and indicators 15 and 16 are reset.

Resulting indicators can also be set or reset as a result of a compare (COMP) operation. COMP is an instruction to compare factor 1 with factor 2. If factor 1 is larger than factor 2, set the HI indicator specified in columns 54 and 55; if factor 1 is smaller than factor 2, set the LO indicator specified in columns 56 and 57; if equal to, the EQ indicator specified in columns 58 and 59.

For example, on line 3 of Figure 14-1, indicator 30 is set if the value of field A is greater than the value of field B, indicator 31 is set if field A is equal to field B, and indicator 32 is set if A is less than B.

So far, factor 1 and factor 2 have always been specified by means of field names—names associated with memory locations in which the values on which to operate can be found. However, factors may also be specified as *literals*—actual values rather than the locations where the values can be found. Just as there are two types of fields, alphabetic and numeric, there are two types of literals, alphabetic and numeric. Field names, alphabetic literals, and numeric literals are distinguished by the RPG on the basis of the following characteristics. A field name always begins with an alphabetic, an alphabetic literal is always enclosed in apostrophes, and a numeric literal always begins with either a number, a minus sign, or a decimal point. Thus, the constants used on the Output Form are really a case of an alphabetic literal.

Lines 4 and 5 of Figure 14-1 give an example of an alphabetic and a numeric literal, respectively. In line 4 a field named SEX is being investigated to see if it contains an alphabetic M for male. If it does, resulting indicator 50 is set; otherwise, resulting indicator

55 is set. In line 5 a field named CLAIM is reduced by $50 before payment is made, an operation that might be performed for a group insurance application incorporating a $50 deductible clause.

A numeric literal must be made up exclusively of numbers, with the sole possible exceptions of the inclusion of one minus sign and/or one period. The period, if included, is not considered part of the literal but is used only to indicate to the RPG where the decimal point is to be assumed to appear. If no period is included, the RPG assumes that the literal is a whole number with no fractional part. If a literal is to be a negative value, it is preceded by a minus sign.

Another calculation operation is MOVE (move to the result the value of factor 2). For example, if the value of ORIG is 'ABCDE', then after the execution of the MOVE operation shown on line 6 of Figure 14-1, the value of DEST is also 'ABCDE'.

Two other calculation operations are SETON and SETOF. They are used, respectively, to set and reset indicators. As many as three indicators may be set or reset with one SETON or SETOF operation. The indicators are specified in columns 54 through 59. For example, line 7 of Figure 14-1 sets the OF indicator and indicators 60 and 70. Line 8 resets the MR indicator and indicator 80.

EXERCISES

Write calculation lines to do the following:

1. Divide a field named DEND by minus three; halfadjust the result and set indicator 20 if the quotient is less than zero, 21 if it is zero, and 22 if it is positive.

2. Compare a field named EYES with the alphabetic characters BLUE, and, if they are equal, set indicator 36; if they are not, set 37.

3. Move zeros into a field named ACCUM.

4. Set indicators 42 and 43.

5. Reset indicator 2.

15 MISCELLANY

The numbered indicators, 01 through 99, may also be used as *field indicators*. Like the OF, 1P, level, record, MR, resulting, and LR indicators, a field indicator can be used to condition calculation and output operations. A field indicator is set according to the value of an input field, and like a resulting indicator, once a field indicator is set it remains set until a subsequent operation resets it.

Field indicators are specified in columns 65 through 70 of the Input Form. If the field with which the field indicators are associated is numeric, a field indicator can be set if the field has a positive, negative, or zero value. If the field is alphabetic, a field indicator can be set if the field contains all spaces. Thus, on the Input Form in Figure 15-1

1. If the value of the NUMBER field is positive, indicator 90 is set, and indicators 91 and 92 are reset.
2. If the value of NUMBER is negative, indicator 91 is set, and indicators 90 and 92 are reset.
3. If the value is zero, indicator 92 is set, and indicators 90 and 91 are reset.

RPG INPUT FORM

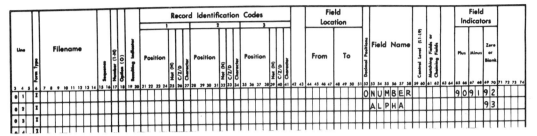

Figure 15-1 Field indicators.

4. If the ALPHA field contains all spaces, indicator 93 is set.

5. If ALPHA contains anything other than all spaces, indicator 93 is reset.

Field indicators are set and reset, not at the time the record containing the associated fields is read, but at the time the record is made available for processing (see Figure 7-7).

15-2 MULTIPLE INPUTS

Chapter 9 described the use of the RPG with two input files. The RPG can be used to program applications with more than two input files. In such a case, one of the files is designated as the primary file and the other files are designated as secondary files. This designation is made on the File Description Form. The secondary file listed first on the File Description Form is the *first secondary file*, the secondary file listed second is the *second secondary file*, the secondary file listed third is the *third secondary file*, and so on.

Multiple input files can be merged in ascending or descending sequence. If ascending, an A is entered for each input file in column 18 of the File Description Form. If descending, a D is entered in column 18 of the File Description Form. When merging files, the RPG object program checks each input file to ascertain that it is in sequence. If any break in sequence is detected, the object program stops on an error indication.

The key field on which multiple input files are merged may consist of as many as three different fields. Thus, the key can be considered as consisting of three subkeys—a major key, an intermediate key, and a minor key. The major key is designated on the Input Form by entering M3 in columns 61 and 62, the intermediate key is designated by entering M2 in columns 61 and 62, and the minor key is designated by entering M1.

When merging multiple input files, the MR indicator is set as long as the key of the current record from any of the secondary files is equal to the key of the last processed primary file record. If two secondary files have equal keys, the RPG object program processes all the records containing this key from the lower numbered secondary file first.

15-3 SEQUENCE CHECKING

Even with an application involving only one input file, the entry of M3, M2, and M1 in columns 61 and 62 of the Input Form can be used to define a key on which the RPG object program is to check the file for either ascending or descending sequence as specified in column 18 of the description of the input file on the File Description Form.

15-4 EDITING

The purpose of this section is to discuss and give examples of some features of edit words that have not previously been touched on in this book.

15-4-1 Check Protection

If instead of a zero an asterisk is used as the significance start character in an edit word, then instead of zero suppressing a field being put out under the control of this edit word, the field is *check protected*. That is, instead of replacing the leading zeros of the field with spaces, they are replaced with asterisks. The difference in effect of a zero significance start character and an asterisk significance start character is exemplified in Table 15-1.

15-4-2 Status

Up to this point in this book all edit words have consisted of only that part of an edit word that is known as the *body* of the edit word,

Table 15-1

| | EDITED VALUE | |
| | Edit word of ' 0' | Edit word of ' *' |
Value		
12345	12345	12345
02345	2345	*2345
00345	345	**345
00045	45	***45
00005	5	****5
00000		*****

the body possibly being followed by one or more other characters. The body of an edit word is that portion that begins with the left-most character of the edit word and continues to the right to the character controlling the transfer of the units position of the data field to the output area.

Following the body in an edit word may be the *status* of the edit word. The status of an edit word is that portion that begins immediately to the right of the body and continues through the credit symbol (CR) or minus sign. The status is optional—it may be present or absent. Following the status of an edit word, or if there is no status, following the body, may be one or more other characters. The following are some sample edit words for a seven-digit data field. In these examples, the body and status of the edit words are marked off.

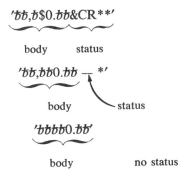

'ƀƀƀƀƀƀ0&***'

body   no status

The property of the status of an edit word is that it appears unchanged in the output if the data field being edited contains a negative value, but it is replaced by fill characters if the data field being edited is not negative. The *fill character* is space if the significance start character is a zero and asterisk if the significance start character is an asterisk. Given the following edit word,

'ƀ,ƀ$0.ƀƀ&CRƀ**'

the values in Table 15-2 would be edited as shown.

Table 15-2

Value	Edited value		
+123456	$1,234.56		**
−123456	$1,234.56	CR	**
+003456	$34.56		**
−003456	$34.56	CR	**
+000000	$.00		**

If an edit word consists of a body and a status followed by other characters, the other characters are produced unchanged in the output. If an edit word consists of a body followed by other characters, the other characters are produced unchanged in the output, except that if any of the other characters are ampersands, the ampersands are replaced by spaces in the output.

15-5 SEQUENCE OF EXECUTION

Calculations and output can be done at detail time and at total time. On both the Calculation and the Output Forms, all the operations to be done at detail time should be entered on the form before any of the operations to be done at total time. Also, for all calculation or output operations to be done at detail time or total time, the operations should be listed on the form in the order in which it is desired to have the RPG object program execute them.

In this book no RPG-programmed example using magnetic-tape input or output has been shown. Although a magnetic-tape handler is a different input device than a punched-card reader and a different output device than a printer, they are all functionally the same— they are all sequential access devices. Thus, magnetic-tape input is not programmed in a way markedly different from the programming for punched-card input, nor is magnetic-tape output programmed in a manner markedly different from the programming for printed output. To a significant extent, once you have learned to program for one sequential access device, you have learned to program for them all.

15-6 MAGNETIC-TAPE INPUT AND OUTPUT

EXERCISES

1. If an input field named INPUT is negative, indicator 1 is to be set; if it is zero, 2 is to be set; if positive, 3. Show how this would be indicated on an Input Form.

2. A 12-digit dollar-and-cents field is to be edited with a decimal point and commas, is to have a floating dollar sign, and is to be check protected. If the value is negative, the characters CR are to be printed following the field but are to be separated from the field by one space. The whole printed field is always to be followed by two asterisks. Write the required edit word.

16 EXAMPLE

A daily stock status listing and summary card updating are to be prepared using the following cards in sequence by part number.

1. Stock status balance cards containing bin quantity, on-order quantity, available quantity, usage last year, usage this year, and so on
2. On-order cards that increase the on-order quantity and the available quantity
3. Receipt cards that increase the bin quantity and decrease the on-order quantity
4. Issue cards that decrease bin quantity and available quantity and increase the usage-this-year quantity

A detail line is printed for each input card. An updated stock status summary card is calculated and, on a change in part number, printed and punched. If the total available quantity is less than or equal to the reorder point, an order card must also be calculated and punched. Figure 16-1 shows the pattern of data flow, and Figures

EXAMPLE   155

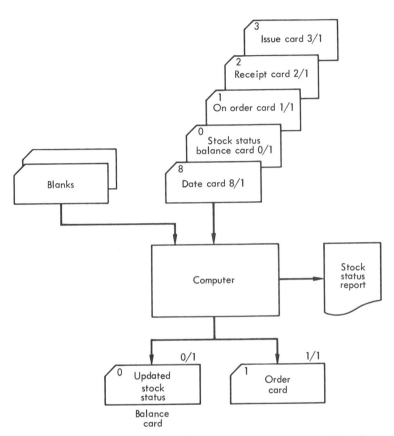

Figure 16-1   Stock status report data flow.

16-2 and 16-3 show the input and output card formats. Figures 16-4
through 16-7 illustrate the completed forms.

**16-1
PROCEDURE**

1. Sequence check by part number.
2. Check that each part number group has only one stock
   status balance input card.
3. Certain fields from the stock status balance card (Table
   16-1) are accumulated for summary card punching and

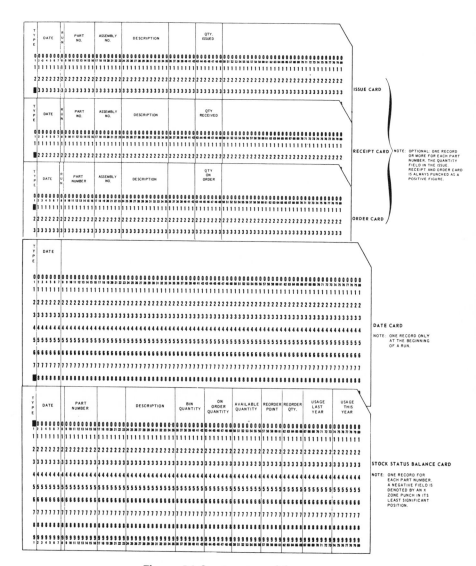

Figure 16-2 Input card formats.

printing. Part number (columns 9–16) and description (columns 24–35) are stored for summary card punching. Reorder point (columns 57–61), reorder quantity (columns 62–66), and usage last year (columns 67–73) are to be stored for printing and summary card punching.

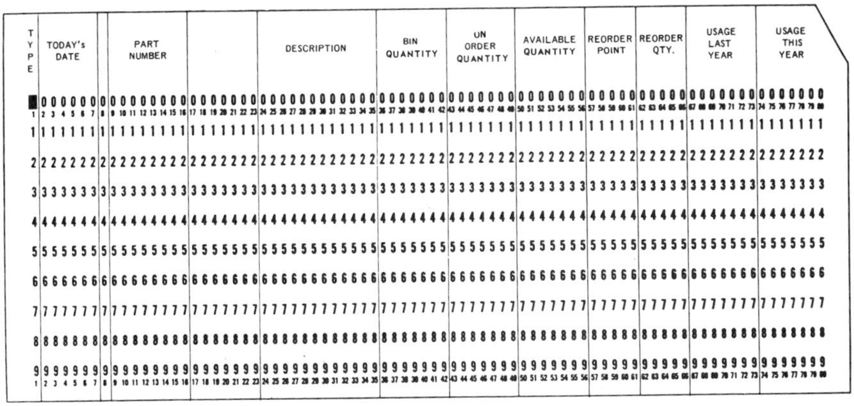

EXAMPLE   **157**

UPDATED STOCK STATUS BALANCE CARD

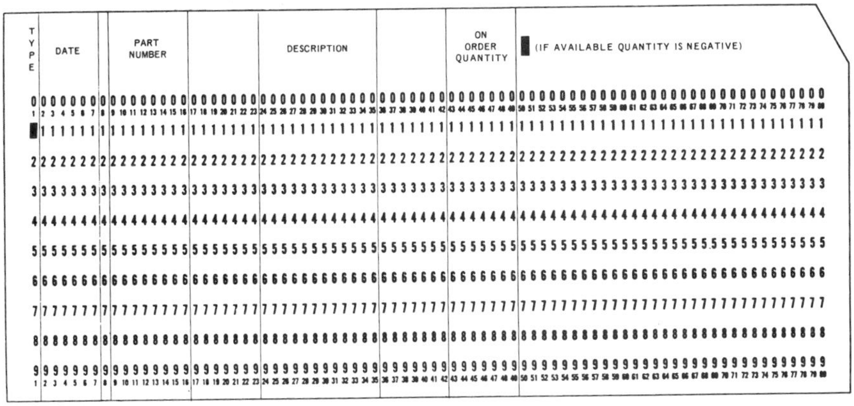

ORDER CARD (ONLY IF REPLENISHMENT IS NECESSARY)

Figure 16-3 Output card formats.

Table 16-1

Type quantity	Card columns
Bin quantity	36–42
On-order quantity	43–49
Available quantity	50–56
Usage this year	74–80

4. The on-order quantity (columns 43–49) from the on-order card is added to the summary card totals of on-order and available quantity.

5. Quantity received (columns 43–49) from the receipt card is added to the summary card total of bin quantity and subtracted from the summary card total of on-order quantity.

6. Quantity issued (columns 43–49) from the issue card is treated as follows.

   (a) It is subtracted from the summary card total of bin quantity.

   (b) It is subtracted from the summary card total of available quantity.

   (c) It is added to the summary card total of usage this year.

7. When a change in part number occurs, the summary card total of available quantity is compared to the reorder point field. If the available quantity is less than or equal to the reorder point, the following calculation is performed and an order card produced.

$$\text{quantity to be ordered} = \text{reorder point} + \text{reorder quantity} - \text{available quantity}$$

If an order card is produced, quantity to be ordered must also be printed in print positions 74–80. If the accumulated available quantity is negative, an asterisk is placed in print position 60 of the stock status report.

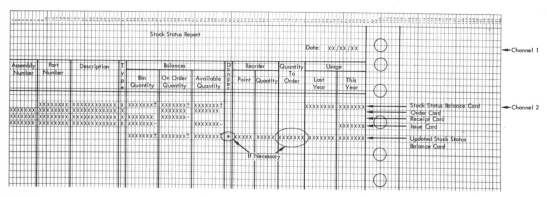

Figure 16-4 Daily stock status report format.

EXAMPLE 159

The layout of this report is shown in Figure 16-4.

1. The report header line consists of the current date from the date card.
2. The stock status balance input card is to be printed as shown on line 13 of Figure 16-4.
3. Designated information from the on-order card, the receipt card, and issue card are printed as shown on lines 14, 15, and 16, respectively. The on-order card quantity field is printed as a positive quantity in print positions 42–48 and 51–57 of line 14. The receipt card quantity field is printed as a positive quantity in print positions 33–39 and as a negative quantity in print positions 42–48 (line 15). Issue card quantity field is printed as a negative quantity in print positions 90–96 (line 16).
4. The updated stock status balance line is printed as shown on line 18 of Figure 16-4.

16-2 DESCRIPTION OF THE STOCK STATUS REPORT TEXT

16-3 FILE SPECIFICATIONS

The File Description Form specifies the file name of the input file and the two output files. The device associated with each file is specified. (The device designated as READ42 is a card punch.) The entry A under sequence indicates that the input file is in ascending order. This specification is related to the M1 entries on the Input Format Specifications form.

RPG FILE DESCRIPTION FORM

Line	Form Type	Filename	File Type	File Designation	End of File	Sequence		Record Length		Key Field Starting Location	Extension Code E/L	Device	
0 1	F	INPUT	I	P		A						READ01	
0 2	F	PRINT	O									PRINTER	
0 3	F	PUNCH	O									READ42	
0 4	F												
0 5	F												

Figure 16-5 Inventory file description.

16-4
INPUT
SPECIFICATIONS

1. Lines 1 and 2 specify the date card. Notice the entry of AA in columns 15 and 16 of line 1. Entries in these *sequence columns* are normally used to describe card type sequences to the RPG, which is done by entering numbers in these columns. (For example, see the discussion of Figure 8-2.) However, the RPG language requires for each record description that if the sequence columns are not used to describe a card type sequence by the entry of numbers, then alphabetics must be entered in these columns. Thus, the AA.

2. Lines 3–13 are the specifications for the input stock status balance card. The 1 in column 17 of line 3 will check that there is only one stock status balance card for each part number group. A level 1 control break (L1) occurs upon a change in part number. Part number is also sequence checked (M1). If the available quantity field (SAVAIL) is negative, field indicator 17 is turned on.

3. The OR relationship is used on lines 14–21 to describe the on-order, receipt, and issue cards because all three records have the same fields in the same positions. Since part number is also specified on these card types, the L1 and M1 entries are made on line number 18. Note that where processing permits, identical fields on all card types have been given a common name.

16-5
CALCULATION
SPECIFICATIONS

1. Lines 1 and 2 specify the calculations for the on-order card.
2. Lines 3 and 4 specify the calculations for the receipt card.
3. Lines 5–7 specify the calculations for the issue card.
4. Lines 8–10 specify the calculations executed at total time.

NOTE: Resulting indicator 17 represents a negative available quantity and is used to control output. Also, resulting indicator 16 is turned on when the available quantity is less than or equal to the reorder point. When this indicator is on, lines 9 and 10 are executed.

RPG INPUT FORM

Line	Form Type	Filename	Sequence	Number (1-N)	Option (O)	Resulting Indicator	Record Identification Codes Position 1	Not (N)	C/Z/D	Character	Position 2	Not (N)	C/Z/D	Character	Position 3	Not (N)	C/Z/D	Character	Field Location From	To	Decimal Positions	Field Name	Control Level (L1-L9)	Matching Fields or Chaining Fields	Field Indicators Plus	Minus	Zero or Blank
01	I	INPUT	AA		08		1		C	8																	
02	I																		2	70		DATE					
03	I		01	1	10		1		C	O																	
04	I																		1	10		TYPE					
05	I																		9	16	0	PART	L1	M1			
06	I																		24	35		DESC					
07	I																		36	42	0	SBIN					
08	I																		43	49	0	SORDER					
09	I																		50	56	0	SAVAIL				17	
10	I																		57	61	0	SPOINT					
11	I																		62	66	0	SQTY					
12	I																		67	73	0	SLAST					
13	I																		74	80	0	STHIS					
14	I		02	N	01		1		C	1																	
15	I		OR		02		1		C	2																	
16	I		OR		03		1		C	3																	
17	I																		1	10		TYPE					
18	I																		9	16	0	PART	L1	M1			
19	I																		17	23	0	NUM					
20	I																		24	35		DESC					
21	I																		43	49	0	QTY					
	I																										
	I																										

Figure 16-6   Inventory input specifications.

RPG CALCULATION FORM

Line	Form Type	Control Level (L0-L9, LR)	Indicators Not	And Not	And Not	Factor 1	Operation	Factor 2	Result Field	Field Length	Decimal Positions	Half Adjust (H)	Resulting Indicators Plus	Minus	Zero or Blank	Compare High 1>2	Low 1<2	Equal 1=2
01	C		01			QTY	ADD	SORDER	SORDER									
02	C		01			QTY	ADD	SAVAIL	SAVAIL									17
03	C		02			QTY	ADD	SBIN	SBIN									
04	C		02			SORDER	SUB	QTY	SORDER									
05	C		03			SBIN	SUB	QTY	SBIN									
06	C		03			SAVAIL	SUB	QTY	SAVAIL									17
07	C		03			QTY	ADD	STHIS	STHIS									
08	C	L1				SAVAIL	COMP	SPOINT								16	16	
09	C	L1	16			SPOINT	SUB	SAVAIL	ORQTY	7	0							
10	C	L1	16			SQTY	ADD	ORQTY	ORQTY									
11	C																	
12	C																	
13	C																	
14	C																	

Figure 16-7   Inventory calculations specifications.

1. Lines 1–3 of page 1 provide for the printing of the date at the top of each page.
2. Lines 4–12 of page 1 provide for the printing of the input stock status balance card.
3. Lines 13–25 of page 1 and line 1 of page 2 provide for the printing of the on-order, receipt, and issue cards.
4. Lines 2–8 of page 2 provide for the punching of an order card only if indicator 16 is on. An 11 punch will be placed in column 50 of the card if the available quantity is negative.
5. Lines 9–20 of page 2 provide for the punching of the updated stock status balance card.
6. Lines 21–25 of page 2 and 1–5 of page 3 provide for the printing of the updated stock status totals. An asterisk (*) is printed in print position 60 if the available quantity is negative. Quantity to be ordered is printed in print positions 74–80 if an order card has been punched.

Notice the entry of H in column 15 of line 1 and the entry of D in column 15 of lines 4 and 13 of page 1 of Figure 16-8. Entries in this column are normally used to distinguish records that are to be produced at total time from records that are to be produced at detail time. (For example, see the discussion of Figure 7-9.) However, the RPG language requires an entry of H, D, or T in column 15 for each output record description. Therefore, H is normally entered for a heading line, and D is entered for all other detail time records.

Also notice the entry of 2 in column 16 of line 9 of page 2 of Figure 16-8. This entry indicates *stacker selection.* In many cases, a card punch has more than one output stacker. In such instances, one of the stackers is called the *normal stacker,* and it is into this normal stacker that cards punched by the punch go unless the punch is directed to do otherwise. The direction consists of instructing the punch to *select* the card into a stacker other than the normal one.

As indicated in Figure 16-1, it is desired to have the updated stock status balance cards in a deck distinct from the order cards.

EXAMPLE   **163**

RPG OUTPUT DESCRIPTION FORM

Line	Form Type	Filename	Type (H/D/T)	Stacker Select	Space Before	Space After	Skip Before	Skip After	Output Indicators And	And	Field Name	Zero Suppress (Z) / Blank After (B)	End Position in Output Record	Constant or Edit Word
01	O	PRINT	H		0 1	0 2			0F					
02	O		OR						08					
03	O										DATE		94	'O / / '
04	O	PRINT	D	1					10					
05	O										PART	Z	16	
06	O										DESC		29	
07	O										TYPE		31	
08	O										SBIN		40	' O- '
09	O										SORDER		49	' O- '
10	O										SAVAIL		58	' O- '
11	O										SLAST	Z	88	
12	O										STHIS	Z	96	
13	O	PRINT	D	1					01					
14	O		OR						02					
15	O		OR						03					
16	O										NUM	Z	7	
17	O										PART	Z	16	
18	O										DESC		29	
19	O										TYPE		31	
20	O								N O1		QTY	Z	39	
21	O								N O3		QTY	Z	48	
22	O								N O2		QTY	Z	57	
23	O								03		QTY	Z	96	
24	O								03				40	' - '
25	O								02				49	' - '

Figure 16-8, page 1   Inventory output specifications.

Since the description of the order card on the Output Form does not specify a stacker, order cards go to the normal stacker, which on the device named READ42 is the stacker numbered 1. The 2 in column 16 of the updated stock status balance card description indicates that updated stock status balance cards are to be selected into the stacker numbered 2 of device READ42. Consequently, when program execution is complete, the punch will have produced two decks, one in stacker 1 and one in stacker 2; all the order cards will be in the deck in stacker 1; and all the updated stock status balance cards will be in the deck in stacker 2.

RPG OUTPUT DESCRIPTION FORM

Line	Form Type	Filename	Type (H/D/T)	Output Indicators	Field Name	Zero Suppress	End Position in Output Record	Constant or Edit Word
0 1	O			03			58	' - '
0 2	O	PUNCH	T	L1 16				
0 3	O						1	' 1 '
0 4	O				DATE		7	
0 5	O				PART		16	
0 6	O				SDESC		35	
0 7	O				ORQTY		49	
0 8	O			17			50	' - '
0 9	O	PUNCH	T2	L1				
1 0	O						1	' 0 '
1 1	O				DATE		7	
1 2	O				PART		16	
1 3	O				DESC		35	
1 4	O				SBIN		42	
1 5	O				SORDER		49	
1 6	O				SAVAIL		56	
1 7	O				SPOINT		61	
1 8	O				SQTY		66	
1 9	O				SLAST		73	
2 0	O				STHIS		80	
2 1	O	PRINT	T 12	L1				
2 2	O				SBIN		40	' 0- '
2 3	O				SORDER		49	' 0- '
2 4	O				SAVAIL		58	' 0- '
2 5	O			17			60	' * '

Figure 16-8, page 2   Inventory output specifications.

RPG OUTPUT DESCRIPTION FORM

Line	Form Type	Filename	Type (H/D/T)	Output Indicators	Field Name	Zero Suppress	End Position in Output Record	Constant or Edit Word
0 1	O				SPOINT	Z	66	
0 2	O				SQTY	Z	72	
0 3	O			16	ORQTY	Z	80	
0 4	O				SLAST	Z	88	
0 5	O				STHIS	Z	96	
0 6	O							
0 7	O							
0 8	O							

Figure 16-8, page 3   Inventory output specifications.

EXAMPLE   165

EXERCISE

A card deck is made up of employee cards and time cards. Employee cards are type 1 cards, time cards are type 2. The deck is in order by employee number. All time cards pertaining to an employee follow the associated employee card in the deck. There may be one or more time cards for each employee card. The layout of the employee card is as follows:

Columns	Fields
1	Type
2–6	Employee number
7–36	Name
37–40	Hourly pay rate in tenths of a cent
41, 42	Number of dependents
43–49	Year-to-date gross pay in cents
50–55	Year-to-date withholding tax in cents
55–60	Year-to-date FICA earnings in cents
61–65	Year-to-date FICA tax in cents
66–70	Quarter-to-date FICA tax in cents

The deck is preceded by a date card with the month in columns 1 and 2, the day in columns 3 and 4, and the year in columns 5 and 6. For each employee, print a check as shown in Figure 16-9 and punch an updated employee-card.

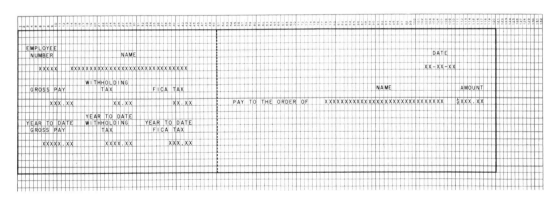

Figure 16-9 Paycheck layout.

INDEX